PRAISE FOR
A DARKER SHADE OF PALE

"Besides offering a searing yet dispassionate account of life in cruel, unforgiving South Africa during Apartheid, A Darker Shade of Pale is an unforgettable love story that will bring tears to your eyes and hope to all those struggling for a better life."
— Philip Berk, eight times past President of the Hollywood Foreign Press Assn.

"I could not put this book down. A Darker Shade of Pale is exceptionally well-written and the prose is delightful. Beryl's memory is amazing. Her vivid sketch of everyday life on the Cape Flats, and the honesty with which she writes are truly compelling."
— Jonathan Jansen, Distinguished Professor of Education, Stellenbosch University, South Africa

"A Darker Shade of Pale is a captivating memoir, but more than that, it is a historical document. The book is an important contribution to the body of literature on life under apartheid because it records the personal experience of those classified as "coloured" under that depraved regime."
— Günther Simmermacher, Editor-in-Chief of The Southern Cross, South Africa.

A DARKER
SHADE OF PALE

Beryl Crosher-Segers

Torchflame Books
An imprint of Light Messages

Durham, NC

Published 2018, by Torchflame Books
    an Imprint of Light Messages
www.lightmessages.com
Durham, NC 27713 USA
SAN: 920-9298

Paperback ISBN: 978-1-61153-280-7
E-book ISBN: 978-1-61153-279-1
Library of Congress Control Number: 2018932652

Author photo by Nev Young

This book is dedicated to

Sarah and Benjamin, my parents,
without whom there would be no story.
My mother with gratitude
for that irreplaceable gift of an education.
Christopher, the one who taught me how to love.
Sasha and Michelin, my heart belongs to you.
Lisa, for honouring our story.
Chelsea, Charlotte, Joshua and Alexander,
you inspired me to write our story.
Maureen and Andy, the inner circle.
In memory of my siblings who have died:
Frances, George and Owen.

"Education is the most powerful weapon which you can
use to change the world." – Nelson Mandela

FOREWORD

Family is everything. In its messy, emotional way the concept permeates our lives and makes us who we ultimately are. In this compelling story, we meet the Croshers, coming together from international beginnings and forming a bonded unit in the dusty parts of Cape Town. It is a time in South Africa's history that is dominated by the white minority's obsession with segregating people by skin colour. I know it well. Like Beryl, I grew up with that burden, the sense of never being good enough, always deemed second-class in a society dominated by what the white elite demanded. And got.

Reading this manuscript made me feel, at times, angry and frustrated as it brought back many of those memories. Some of them had been neatly packaged and stored in the far recesses of my subconscious, never needing to be accessed and certainly not pleasant. I remember, as Beryl does, being denied service in a restaurant, in my case near Bloemfontein, and told to go round the back to buy take-aways at a window. I remember only too well as a child not understanding why some kids could go on the dodgem cars on Durban's beachfront but not I. I remember with fervid anger having to apply for special permission to attend university because I was the "wrong" colour.

These memories make me bristle even today, decades later, and having enjoyed the benefits of living for almost twenty years in my new home in Australia, free of the legislated racial discrimination that had dominated my formative years. It was here, for the first time in my life, that I was made to feel that my most significant defining factor was NOT the colour of my skin. That took a bit of getting used to, having had it drummed into me over a long period of time that being an oppressed, brown-skinned person was the most I could aspire to being.

It was a world, almost unimaginable by today's standards, in which every aspect of daily life was determined by racial classification. The haves and the have-nots. And sandwiched between these two competing demographics of white and black were our designated group, the Cape Coloured. The misfits, the mixed ones that didn't neatly fit into either camp, but drew from both. We were not as badly treated as black Africans, who were oppressed in the most brutal way, but at the same time fell well short of joining the "haves". We were, as the title of this book implies, too fair-skinned to be black, and too dark-skinned to be white. We hovered somewhere in the grey limbo.

It would be very tempting to describe this as a memoir about apartheid, which looms large in the emotional landscape we traverse with Beryl. It is not. It certainly describes the day-to-day humiliations, the cries from the heart about the injustice of being treated like a victim of racial discrimination (not just in the law, but, more importantly, in people's attitudes).

No, ultimately, it is about the ties that bind.

In this case, the focus is on an impoverished family that clings together through good times and the darkest of days. We endure with them the hardship of feeding six hungry mouths (the adults eat last), of sharing a tiny council house where water has to be heated in a pot before anyone can have a bath and some of the kids have to sleep in the lounge-room because there's simply nowhere else to put them. We meet the neighbours who, like an extended family, step in to help with a plate of biscuits here, a freshly slaughtered chicken there. They form a community. Nowhere is it illustrated more poetically than in the way the whole street turns out to pay its respects when a family member dies in the most tragic of circumstances. Or, to share in the joy when a bride leaves her family home at age 20 to start a new life.

There is, running through this book like a vein carrying life-blood, a strong urge to take risks, to explore, to experience. Sometimes it ends in tears. And often it manifests itself in simple ways, such as daring people of colour to sit on benches legally reserved for white South Africans. Or in more complex situations: mixing socially and politically with other races when there was a personal price to pay.

Perhaps the greatest risk was the family's decision to seek a better life somewhere else. Somewhere that wasn't South Africa, that didn't force their children – the next generation – into the same destructive racial confines that had held the parents and the grandparents back. But risks are by their nature fraught with emotional displacement. I know this from my own experience, having made the same decision sometime later – to leave the country of my birth and start from scratch in a new place. It was the most painful decision of my life, knowing what I was leaving behind but filled with uncertainty about what prospects, if any, lay ahead.

Imagine doing that – selling up and packing your belongings – with a young family. And being four months pregnant. That's the way Beryl starts the Australian adventure that, with a few explosive twists and turns, becomes the focus of her life. It's in those twists and turns that the true value of her story comes to life. But I won't try to encapsulate the thrust of it. After all, Beryl does that best.

Anton Enus, January 2018

ACKNOWLEDGEMENTS

My deepest gratitude goes to the people who encouraged me to write my story.

I feel privileged to be the one to record our family history. These stories have been passed on to me from my parents, relatives and through recollections of my childhood memories. I acknowledge with respect and appreciation the many people who shared their stories, and offered support and encouragement.

To my editor, Natasha Gilmour, who rescued me when I was in the depths of despair. You are the angel sent to guide my book with your gentle hands. You are a true professional and I share this book with you.

Warren Ludski, a man with a commitment to the stories of our people. Thank you for reading my manuscript at short notice and for the valuable feedback.

To documentary-maker Bebi Zekirovski, who quietly stepped into my path and offered support and encouragement.

My friend Leisl Baumgartner, thank you for being a champion of this book.

To the Light Messages team, a thousand thank-yous for acknowledging my debut manuscript and for everything you've done to bring this story to print.

My thanks to Anton Enus who so generously agreed to read my manuscript and to write a foreword that moved me to tears.

I remain forever grateful to Philip Berk for his encouraging review and for remaining a faithful correspondent over the years.

A massive thanks to Günther Simmermacher, whose review, supportive comments and insightful edits helped raise my confidence to another level.

Thank you and love to my cousins, friends and dedicated social media followers (too many to mention by name but you know who you are) for being pillars of strength.

To my nephews and nieces and their families, I hope this book gives a valuable insight into our family history.

I am grateful to my daughter-in-law Lisa who so eagerly read my manuscript and offered her support throughout this journey.

To my darling grandsons Joshua and Alexander, I hope that one day you will find this story of value.

My love to my precious granddaughters Chelsea and Charlotte for keeping this story alive with readings and questions.

Sasha and Michelin, you have been my rocks. When those signs on benches and trains dictated your life path, we knew that you deserved a better life. I hope this book gives you an insight into the sacrifices Dad and I made to ensure that you and our future generations could grow up in a society free of legislated racial discrimination. We are handing over the reigns to you to keep our heritage alive.

Christopher, I will be forever grateful for your never-failing encouragement. Thank you for loving me despite my many failings on the domestic front. Thank you for the endless cups of coffee, listening to my long talks, my anger and tears, and for always finding a solution to my problems.

Mum, Maureen and Andy, we are the only ones left of the inner circle. We are forever joined by the blood that pumps in our veins. Our love for each other holds us close, no matter where we find ourselves.

CONTENTS

Foreword vii
Acknowledgements xi
Abroad 1
    Sydney, Australia: August 1982,
        Mid-Winter 1
    Retreat, South Africa: November 1982,
        Late Spring 3
The Beginning 10
    Cape Town, South Africa: 1959,
        Mid-Summer 10
Owen's Star 27
    Darling, South Africa: January 1962,
        Mid-Summer 27
    Steenberg, South Africa: January 1963,
        Summer 36
Division 39
    Steenberg, South Africa: January 1965,
        Mid-Summer 54
Community and Faith 57
The Red Wireless 68
    Steenberg, South Africa: September 1966,
        Early Spring 68

Apartheid Intensified...................................... 97
   Steenberg, South Africa: January 1972,
      Mid-Summer 97
A White Society.. 119
   South Africa: January 1973,
      Mid-Summer 119
Christopher 128
   South Africa: August 1973,
      Early Spring.................................... 128
Goodbye Dad 133
   Home, South Africa: July 1974,
      Mid-Winter.................................... 133
Segregated Life 149
   Cape Town, South Africa: Early 1975,
      Summer.. 155
Wedding Plans 161
Political Chaos 174
Flight to Freedom.. 186
   South Africa: August 1980,
      Late Winter 186
   Sydney, Australia: July 1982,
      Late Winter 198
Home Calling 204
   Retreat, South Africa: November 1982,
      Late Spring 204
Stateless and Flagless.................................. 221
   Sydney, Australia: August 1988,
      Late Winter 221
Little Coloured Boy 227
   Dear Dad,...................................... 235
About the Author 244

1

ABROAD

SYDNEY, AUSTRALIA: AUGUST 1982, MID-WINTER

I couldn't escape the memory of Christopher carrying me over the threshold of our first home. It was a joyous occasion; we were so proud of ourselves and of what we had achieved. At that point we had no intention of leaving South Africa. Now, 18 months later, we had uprooted ourselves, sold our house, our car, and left secure jobs to seek freedom for our children.

We felt exiled. Here, we had nothing. Not even a bed to sleep on.

The stark reality of our situation was sinking in quickly. We had to start again in Australia and it was not easy. We had no friends and knew only my sister Frances and her family. I cried a lot over my fear that we had made the wrong decision. Thoughts of the bigger picture were furthest from my mind. In my pregnant state, the smells in shopping centres made me sick; the wet weather and being out of my comfort zone added to my misery. Frances tried to be accommodating. She even tossed out the air-freshener in the car and replaced it with lemon peels, like we used to do at home, in South Africa.

I constantly felt pangs of homesickness and missed the sight of Table Mountain in Cape Town. I missed our familiar roads. I missed the noise of the children playing outside. I missed our friends and my cousins who regularly visited our house. I longed for the laughter and fun we had when everyone gathered at our house.

Now, I did not care about apartheid and the racist policies of the government in South Africa. I felt happier there.

In Australia, the days were long and lonely. I was depressed and my anxiety surfaced more often. I would panic about not being able to breathe during the birth of our baby. My fears grew about giving birth and not having anyone around to meet our baby. I could not hide my disappointment that this was not what I fantasised about.

This was not my idea of living a life of *freedom*.

Mum had arrived two months later. Her first overseas trip was something she had dreamed of since Frances started talking about going to Australia. It also led to the worst time of her life. She walked right into our misery. We were so unhappy and fixed on every negative aspect of our surroundings—the way people looked, the way they talked, walked—everything was wrong. We missed our many friends and family, our parish, our home—our life, as we knew it.

We announced our plans to return to South Africa.

RETREAT, SOUTH AFRICA: NOVEMBER 1982, LATE SPRING

In the first few weeks back I struggled to settle back into home life. I harboured so many unresolved issues with Mum which only increased my unease about what the future held for *all* of us.

Living in our new house brought us back among our parish community, although this presented its own issues. I found it difficult to field questions about the reasons for our return, how I felt about having sold up everything for want of a better life, only to return. I had to deal with probing questions and listen to people talk about the success of their family members who were abroad.

'So, the grass is not greener on the other side after all,' someone remarked. 'You sold your beautiful home and everything you owned to go to Australia, and now you've come running back to good 'ole Africa,'—those were things regularly said to us.

The parish priest, thankfully, recognised my struggle. Born and raised in the same area I grew up in, he knew many of my family members and he identified with having moved abroad, as he had done as a young man to study for the priesthood. With his encouragement, I immersed myself in parish life and was soon in charge of the weekly newsletter, teaching catechism, and my passion—fundraising.

As time progressed, I befriended many parishioners and felt encouraged by the work they were doing to ensure that impoverished families received food parcels and pastoral care. In particular the sacristan, who had served the parish for many years, and who was the saving grace for many priests, roped me in to work with the seniors' groups and other committees.

My desire to keep the disadvantaged children and young people in our parish engaged led me to producing plays and assisting the fundraising committee. The first big event I became involved in was a Debutante Ball. The very thought of young ladies in the parish dressing up for a ball and organising activities to raise funds caused so much excitement. We had regular meetings at our house and I took a few of the debutantes under my wing to assist them with clothes and fundraising ideas.

It was during one of these fundraising activities that I befriended a well-presented and reserved young man. He had agreed to partner one of the debutantes.

One Saturday afternoon, I answered a knock on our door and found myself face-to-face with him.

'I am sorry to disturb your afternoon, but can I please ask you for some advice?' he said.

'Of course, come inside.'

Drawn and pale he fumbled through a bunch of papers in his hands.

'I don't know how to say this ...' his voice trailed off.

Lowering his gaze, he looked at the handwritten papers. Trying to put him at ease, I laughed and put out my hand to take the papers.

'What is this? An assignment? Love letters?' I said, trying to make light of the situation.

'No, Mrs Segers, I heard that you are a good typist. I need help with typing up some notes my father made,' he said fixing his gaze on our piano.

I scanned the heading on the first page: 'Affidavit', in bold print. When I looked up at him tears had formed in his eyes.

'My father is innocent. This is his affidavit. I need help so that he can present it for his defence.'

'What did your father do?' I asked hesitantly.

'I am not sure if you remember the gruesome murder of a man whose body was found floating in the *vlei* (lake) near the station. My father did not do it.' This time he stared me in the eyes searching my face for a reaction.

I distantly remembered the murder. It was particularly gruesome and people feared for their safety at the time. A man living in our suburb, whose pregnant wife worked at a local factory, had been lured away from home to drive someone to a hospital. He was never seen alive again. The sawmill near Retreat Station was identified as the place where the body was dismembered and then dumped in the vlei. A local resident, who regularly sat close to the vlei to sell her products to passers-by, saw the black bags floating in the water.

Here I was, sitting with the son of one of the accused. A chill ran down my spine but I had to remain calm. He was clearly distressed.

'When do you need this by?' I asked, trying to ease the tension in the room.

'I would really appreciate it if you can do it very soon.'

I was fascinated as I typed the father's account of his whereabouts and his version of events. No one talked about the case, because it had happened a few years earlier, but it was clear that this young man believed in his father's innocence. After giving back the paperwork I never raised the topic with him again. One of the accused had been sentenced to death. His father and another accomplice received jail time. As preparations progressed for the Debutante Ball, I noticed how this remarkable young man blossomed and continued to aspire to reach his goals.

To quell my restlessness, I got more involved in our parish. I formed a strong friendship with our parish priest, Father Gerard Masters. He would visit our home regularly for meals and to discuss parish activities.

Father Masters was a young priest, full of life and different to the many older priests we had over the years. Born and raised in Retreat, he had completed his studies for the priesthood in Rome and returned to South Africa to serve in our parish.

His zest for life, love of beautiful things and youthful outlook ignited our parish, and we embarked on many new projects to uplift our community.

He encouraged me to work with the children in our parish and to get involved in fundraising. This helped me to focus my energies in other areas and to stop fretting about what had happened with our unsuccessful immigration plans. Whenever our discussion turned to Australia, he would find a way to change the mood.

'For now, focus on your daily life,' he said. 'You have many talents and the time will come when things will be clearer. You will know when the time is right to make decisions about your future.'

To further lighten the atmosphere, he would grab the guitar or play our piano and start singing in Italian. He teased the children and lavished them with love and attention. Often, he would cook his favourite Italian recipes in our kitchen. This being what got me through my darkest days.

As fate would have it the second chance for Australia was closer than we knew.

One Sunday, we returned to Cape Town Station after a day wandering around town with the children. As we approached the platform the train was already waiting. When we reached the first carriage, Sasha, our daughter started to complain that she was tired and walked towards the first carriage. Above the window was the "whites only" sign.

I continued, walking a few steps ahead, pushing Michelin in the pram. Behind me I could hear Christopher coaxing Sasha to continue to walk further down to the platform.

'I am too tired,' she cried, walking towards the door of the carriage. 'My legs cannot move anymore.'

'Come, I'll carry you,' Christopher offered, with his arms outstretched.

'No, I am getting in here,' she insisted. 'I want to sit down on those seats now.'

I turned around to look at them. Christopher was kneeling on the ground next to Sasha, explaining that we could not get into that carriage.

'We must walk further down because our carriages are down there.' He pointed towards the other end.

With his shoulders drooped he took her hand and continued walking. We strolled past the first three carriages until we reached the "non-white" sign.

I knew this would become one of many deciding factors for our return to Australia.

My last concert at our parish before we departed again for Australia was a musical called *Psalty, The Singing Songbook*. St Anne's served a large community living in sub-economic housing, and many people were living in the shacks without running water and electricity. The shacks were constructed of old metal sheets and inside they were insulated with newspapers pasted on the walls. A small percentage of the parishioners were home-owners.

It was a vibrant, friendly and nurturing community, thanks to so many people who were determined to make the parish thrive despite the widespread hardships. The musical would form part of St Anne's twenty-fifth anniversary celebrations. No auditions were held and any interested child was welcomed.

Several children who wanted to participate were from Vrygrond, also known as Free Ground. There was nothing free about it. Vrygrond was an open piece of council land along Prince George Drive near the False Bay sea board. The Group Areas Act instrumented the separate development of races in South Africa. It also granted authorisation to forcibly remove non-whites from valuable pieces of land so those could become white settlements. Vrygrond offered displaced coloured families temporary housing while they were on the housing waiting list.

Vrygrond lacked basic amenities such as electricity, running water or sanitary facilities, and it was a breeding ground for many diseases, including tuberculosis. There were very few shared toilets; the council would collect the open sewage only once a week. There was one water tap available to a few hundred people. The place was infested with flies and littered with rubbish.

I cannot accurately articulate the despair and frustration these residents felt. But despite these hardships, many people tried to maintain a normal life. The parents were very eager for their children to participate. Christopher was roped into picking them up and driving them home. Some of the rehearsals were scheduled in the evening because most of the musicians worked during the day. Through the organist in the parish we were fortunate to get some great musicians from the University of Cape Town. As we drew closer to the performance date, in the heart of winter, Christopher would drive into Vrygrond to pick up the children and later drop them back home. The parents would be waiting close to their shacks, with candles burning to guide him to their homes.

I was born in Retreat, five kilometres from Vrygrond. I too, knew displacement. We were no different. In late 1959 we were relocated from Retreat to Steenberg. I remember how, before our letter from council arrived, in the stillness of the morning smoke billowed from open fires near the scattered round huts with grass-covered roofs. The stench of raw meat cooking on open fires filled the air. With no wind to blow it up into the sky, it instead hung over the hills like a mist, filling our nostrils with the nauseating smell.

People would move quietly between the big black pots and the huts, stopping to talk to each other, and occasionally women bent over to adjust and tighten the blankets holding the babies on their backs. Old men sat around the fires smoking their pipes or getting up to throw pieces of wood on the fire or to stoke it with a long pole which caused sparks to fly out.

Near the huts children laughed and played, talking in Xhosa, one of South Africa's indigenous languages.

2

THE BEGINNING

CAPE TOWN, SOUTH AFRICA: 1959, MID-SUMMER

Growing up in the southern suburbs of Cape Town at 10th Avenue, Retreat, our summer days were spent running around barefoot on the sand dunes behind our house with our cousins and neighbourhood children.

The hills, ablaze with wildflowers and scattered trees, stretched for miles. In the pond at the foot of the hills, lush green reeds and colourful water lilies filled the murky water, giving shade to the little fish darting around.

Climbing the hill, the soft fine sand covered our feet, clearing our footprints as we hid from each other in the bushes. Shouts of laughter filled the air as we ran down the hill towards the pond to catch tadpoles. Everyone called them *teppels*.

Georgie, my older brother, was six years old at the time, and my older cousins Eddie, Norman and Gene would walk close to the water's edge. Frances, my older sister, was seven years old. She, my cousin Eleanor and I sat among the daisies, making flower chains to wear as a necklace or crowns. Scooping the murky water into glass jars and holding it up to the light, the boys checked for the wriggly *teppels*.

The pond was the dividing line between our place and the so-called *Kaffir Lokasie*, named by the locals as the area for indigenous people, using what has become the worst racial slur one can direct at a black South African.

Close-by, a few goats grazed on the grass around the pond that was surrounded by Port Jackson trees which shielded the huts from the road. In the distance stretched miles of bushes with the tips of the mountains reaching into the blue sky.

Our house was built by my maternal grandfather, Manuel Stebes, who arrived in Saldanha Bay, north-west of Cape Town, in 1904, on a boat from Lisbon. Mum and her 12 sisters and two brothers filled us with many tales of our grandfather's arrival in South Africa. The boat, carrying its cargo and sailors, sunk off the coast. After clinging to parts of the boat, Grandfather Stebes along with three other sailors made it to shore.

A farmer who found the exhausted survivors took them to his farm. My maternal great-grandparents, originally from Mozambique on the south-eastern coast of Africa, worked on the farm where the stricken sailors were cared for. My grandparents' mixed heritage stemmed from bushmen and the Bantu inhabitants of Mozambique. My grandmother, Frances Adonis, grew up on the farm and joined her mother working in the farmer's house.

Manuel fell in love with the young Frances and they later married. They set up home in a place called Grootfontein, a short distance from Saldanha Bay. My grandmother, who was skilled in housework, efficiently set up and managed her new home. My grandfather found work as a stonemason in the nearby town of Hopefield. They lived there until fifteen of their sixteen children were born.

Around 1934, they purchased land in Retreat and my grandfather built a two-bedroomed house there. He then moved the family, twelve daughters and two sons, to Retreat. Born a twin, Mum was the fifth youngest. Her twin brother Manuel died when he was a few months old. The thirteenth daughter was born in Retreat. Mum and her siblings were classified by the government as being of mixed race

My grandmother died at the age of 58. Mum was 16 years old. The family continued to live in the house with my grandfather until his death a year later.

Mum found herself a live-in job at a hotel in Muizenberg on the False Bay Coast. Her older, married, siblings fostered the younger ones who were left behind. Mum and her sister, Aunty Linda, moved back into the house after they both married. I was born in the house in 1955, and my baby brother Owen in 1957.

The house, set at the foot of the sand hills, had a sandstone chimney facing the road. The toilet, in a small room down the back of the property, attracted many flies around the opening of the bucket. Newspaper squares hung on the wire hook behind the door. On hot days, the stench inside the toilet was unbearable, and Mum could not wait for the night soil man to replace the bucket on his weekly collection rounds.

The strong smell of the cleaning liquid Jeyes Fluid was a clear sign that the night soil man had replaced the bucket and might have dropped some of the contents on his walk back to the truck.

On the large property next door, Mum's eldest sister, Aunty Sissie, lived with her granddaughter in a spacious house. The fenced-in, tree-filled property spread over a large area. It also had an outside toilet which we often used.

Because of the big age difference between Mum and her older siblings, Aunty Sissie's children—our first cousins— were closer to Mum's age or older, and already married. Names like Sissie and Tietie for older sisters or Boetie for a younger brother were given as a mark of respect, and as children we addressed them using these names.

The big fig tree in the middle of the yard offered shade from the harsh summer sun. In fig season, the many fruit-laden branches were covered with brown paper bags or nets to keep the birds away. The figs were not for picking and eating. Instead the fruits were used to make jars of fig conserve, called *konfyt*. The sweet smell of the fruit boiling filled the backyard and soon jars filled with sticky fig jam stood cooling in the kitchen.

In watermelon season, after we had devoured the slices of juicy red flesh, Mum saved the left-overs. After removing the rind she would cut them into squares and soak them in a mixture of lime and water for a day or two. After thoroughly rinsing them to remove the lime water, she boiled the squares in a pot filled with water, lemon and sugar. The cooled slices of watermelon conserve, spread on fresh homemade bread, was a special treat.

Dad, classified as mixed race through his East Indian heritage, worked six days a week as a barman at Wynberg Hotel. On Tuesdays, his day off, he sat around reading the newspaper or listening to the radio while drinking wine and rolling tobacco in paper squares to make cigarettes. He had this knack of blowing out perfect circles of smoke at regular intervals. We entertained ourselves running around trying to catch the circles or counting how many butts he dropped into the silver tin. Sometimes he cooked our main meal while Mum sewed.

Frances and Georgie attended St Mary's Primary School in Retreat Road, next to St Mary's Catholic Church. My day was spent playing with my baby brother Owen who now was nearly two years old. In the afternoons, after they returned from school, I would roam the hills with Frances and Georgie in search of discarded meat bones buried by the dogs in the sand. Frances would fill her tin with the bones in exchange for pennies from Mr Johannes, the bottle and bone collector. She would collect the bones left from our meals and scrub them to add to her hidden stash.

Walking down to the shop on the corner, our eyes would be peeled to the ground searching every nook and cranny for bones. Saturday mornings, Frances who was fiercely protective of her tin, waited until she heard the familiar sound of Mr Johannes's horn as he rode in his horse-drawn cart down the avenue. We'd follow Frances, who'd be clutching her tin as she jostled to join the queue. After examining her bones, Mr Johannes would drop one or two pennies in her hand.

In the distance, always perfectly timed, the sound of the ice cream vendor's bell filled the air, tempting Frances to line up again to buy suckers with her pennies. Walking back home, licking our suckers, our eyes would be darting around looking for the elusive bone to start filling the bucket again.

In late 1959, Mum and Dad received that council notice informing them of a new development with the land. This meant that after living happily together for a few years we were forced to move away from our cousins. We were allocated a house in the council housing estate in Steenberg, about five kilometres away.

My cousins moved to a council housing estate in Silvertown, far away from us. After playing with them every day, we were now separated and did not see them again for a long time. On the day we moved, Mum said goodbye to those neighbours who were left waiting to move to other areas. She spent some time walking around the house where she had spent most of her life, and where she had been able to live with her own family.

This was the start of our life in a council housing estate.

We moved to a two-bedroomed semi-detached house in a narrow street lined with blocks of two or four houses. They had distinct grey asbestos roofs. Some houses had one bedroom, others had two or three, based on the rental.

Frances was prim and proper. Her unruly black hair was always tightly pulled back in a neat bun. She had a sprinkling of freckles on her fair skin. All her belongings were neatly packed in her drawers or on the shelf which Mum had made in our room. Frances always helped in the kitchen and would fuss about Owen, dressing him and wiping his face and hands. She made sure that we

15

did things properly, like wearing our socks and shoes, and not make loud noises.

Georgie, just 15 months younger than Frances, was the teaser, often doing the impossible, jumping from one bed to another on one foot as I giggled at his antics. He was good at making up games and riddles and questioned Mum about everything. Georgie could not sit still for very long. He once ventured so close to the fruit and vegetable cart to touch the horse and was lucky that he was just out of reach when the horse reacted by kicking its hind leg, just narrowly missing Georgie.

Owen looked different to us. While we were all dark haired, he had light brown hair and green eyes. A quiet little boy. He would follow Mum around the house or play close to where she often sat at her sewing table in the bedroom.

Frances and I shared a bed, and Georgie slept in his own bed. Owen slept in the pram.

The flat backyard had patches of grass and one big tree near the door. Outside the back-door was a little brick shed where we stored our firewood. In the cramped kitchen, the stove took up most of the space, with limited space for our kitchen table.

Beaming with happiness, Mum opened the tap in the kitchen sink and let the water run over her hands before filling our mugs with water to drink.

We now had more living space than we had in our old house.

'Pull this chain every time you use the toilet,' Mum instructed, demonstrating the action to the four of us gathered around the toilet bowl. Georgie was the first one to have a turn. We watched as the water rose in the toilet bowl and then flowed back to the normal level. We now also had a basin with a tap to wash our hands and to brush our teeth. Behind the door was the hook filled with squares of newspaper.

Mum, pregnant with her fifth child, spent many hours cleaning, painting and clearing the garden. The Cape Flats Development Association (CAFDA), a community centre established in 1944, assisted people living in poverty. They offered second-hand clothing, packaged food and powdered milk. Mum bought remnants of fabric and stitched curtains to cover the windows.

The paint, a white powder mixed with water, filled a bucket. Mum painted the whole house with it. We helped by dipping the paint brushes in and handing them to Mum while she stood on the table to reach the ceiling and the upper parts of the walls.

'Watch Owen, don't let him put his hands in the paint,' Mum reminded us as she wiped the sweat from her eyes.

Frances helped by painting the bottom parts of the walls. When dried, the paint left a powdery residue on the walls, leaving white marks on our clothes if we brushed against it.

Next door to us lived Mr and Mrs Hess and their family. Mrs Hess was housebound with her disabled son and their children soon became our friends.

Early one morning, hearing a newborn's cry in Mum's room, we watched through the crack in the door as the local midwife, Nurse Wichtman, placed our new baby sister Maureen in Mum's arms. Maureen was so tiny with dark brown curly hair and a scrunched-up face. Mrs Hess watched over Mum, wiping her face and holding a cup of water to her lips. We sat near the open door for a while, watching Nurse Wichtman bathe Maureen before dressing her in a teeny baby nightie and wrapping her in a blanket. Dad stood in the kitchen, pressing his pants before getting dressed for work.

The new baby meant a shift in sleeping arrangements. Owen started sharing Georgie's bed and Maureen slept in the pram. Mum was up and out of bed the next day, feeding Maureen, cooking, washing and cleaning.

A few weeks after Maureen was born we walked to the baby clinic close to where we lived at 10th Avenue in Retreat. We stopped in to visit Aunty Sissie who still lived in the big house with a shop in her garage. The shop, classified as a business, allowed Aunty Sissie to remain in her property after it was declared an industrial area. The stone chimney was the only reminder of my grandparents' house. The rest of the house had been demolished. Across the road other properties had been flattened and the land cleared.

Georgie, always ready to go exploring in the sand hills, already had his shoes off. 'Let's go to the pond for *teppels*,' he shouted.

We peeled off our shoes and socks and raced each other to the top of the hills and down the other side to the pond to catch *teppels*. A stillness hung over the hills. The huts were gone, only a big empty space remained. No people. No smoke. No open fires. No goats.

Early one morning in December 1960, Mum was busy packing our belongings into boxes.

'Frances, come and help me pack the clothes into bags, we have to pack up and move to another house. It's not far away and we can walk there.'

Mum and Dad could no longer afford the rent for the two-bedroomed house and we had to move to a one-bedroom house. Mr Jacobs down the street, the owner of an open lorry, moved our furniture. We walked behind Mum with Maureen in the pram to our new house at 30 Chimes Street.

Our new house was much smaller. Mum arranged the house as best she could, making our beds in the lounge room. Racing out of the back door, we climbed over the wire fence and headed to the top of the sand dunes. The sand covered most of the wire fence and stretched as far as my eyes could see.

Georgie often led the way up the hill followed by Frances and me. Squealing with laughter we'd chase each other up and down the hills. Owen, whose little legs were too short for the loose sand, struggled to get to the top, and he would stop half way to wait for one of us to help him.

From the top of the hill we could see over the roof-tops and look down into our backyard where Mum was usually hanging the washing or sweeping the sand away from the door entrance. Maureen would lay in her pram or Mrs Khune would carry her home.

Mr and Mrs Khune, an older childless couple, lived next door in the end house of the block of four. They welcomed us into their home generously, serving plates of cookies and cool drinks. Mrs Khune, petite and softly spoken, had dark skin and slanted eyes. She wore the same hairstyle every day: a beehive covered with a black hair net. She always wore a white apron and pink lipstick. Their lounge, neatly furnished with a special chair for Noddy, the ginger cat, had no beds in it, unlike ours.

The smell of Mrs Khune's food and baked bread drifted into our backyard. Every day she would call Mum to the fence saying, 'This is for the children, Mrs Crosher. I know they are always hungry and this will help to feed them. One loaf of bread is too much for us.'

Mum would gratefully accept the food, as well as the relief Mrs Khune provided by looking after Maureen during the day.

Mr Khune, tall and skinny, had a small head, high-boned cheeks and small beady eyes that twinkled and darted about when he talked or laughed. His workspace in the backyard was filled with paint tins, pieces of timber, sink sheets, empty bottles and tools. He rode his black bicycle to work every day, and every afternoon he'd cover it up with a sheet of canvas. Some afternoons he would give us rides on the handle bars up and down the road.

A great storyteller, his fascinating tales about his childhood would keep us spellbound. Most of his childhood was spent on farmland in Namaqualand, situated along the South African and South West African borders. Mr Khune, a descendant of the Khoisan people, told us many stories about roaming in the bushes and herding cattle. We pictured the miles and miles of open fields filled with colourful daisies. The details about hunting for lizards and moles had us girls squirming, but it made Georgie keen to search the hills for lizards and anything crawling in the bushes.

Skilled at making things for us to play with, Mr Khune carved a wooden gun and a Y-shaped catapult for Georgie. The catapult, or kettie, as Georgie called it, was used to shoot stones at birds and lizards on the hills. In the afternoons Georgie would roam the hills looking for any moving objects to shoot at. Down the hill, we raced holding on to the string tied to the magnificent kites Mr Khune built. His frantic shouts echoed in the hills as he issued instructions for us to balance the kite.

Mr Khune taught us how to spread chicken wire over pieces of timber to trap birds. Skilfully he flattened paraffin tins, then bent and shaped the metal pieces to make sleds. Smoothing the rough edges, Mr Khune bent the edge to form a handle over the front to grip as we slid down the hills.

'This candle wax I am spreading on the bottom will make you slide faster downhill,' he explained. 'And, make sure that you hold onto the handle and lean forward when you slide.'

Mr and Mrs Khune filled our lives with kindness and joy. We loved going next door to play because our tummies were always filled with treats and left-over food. She was like an angel sent to help Mum.

At the other end of our row of houses lived the Dreyer family with their four children. They had been moved from Diep River, an area that had been declared 'white' under the Government's Group Areas Act.

Across the road, lived Mr and Mrs Africa with their large family; they had been moved from Constantia, a picturesque suburb at the foot of the Constantiaberg Mountains. This area, filled with vineyards, was also rezoned 'white' under the Group Areas Act, and the families were moved to the Cape Flats and other non-white areas. Mrs Africa often tearfully talked to Mum about the farm her family lived on before it was declared a white area.

Now, their cramped backyard was filled with chicken pens and a vegetable garden which resembled a small farm. Many other families living in the road had suffered the same fate of forced removals.

We quickly settled down in the neighbourhood. Frances and Georgie, who attended Steenberg No. 2 Primary, walked to school. In the afternoons, as soon as they arrived home, we'd explore the hills, pick berries and sour figs until Mum called us home for supper time.

During the summer holidays, we'd spend the day making caves with tree branches, and in the evenings we sat on the hills drinking homemade ginger beer. In the distance we watched moving images on the big screen at the Sea Breeze Drive-in. Frances and I would sit mes-merised by the characters on the screen. Little did I know that we would *not* be allowed to enter the drive-in because it was for white people only.

'Let's go hunting,' Georgie would call out as soon as he was bored watching the moving images on the distant screen.

The only visitors to our house were the Catholic priest and nuns, who always encouraged Mum to bring us back to the church. Dad, who had been briefly married before, and Mum, for having married a divorced man, were considered as outcasts.

As their children, we were baptised, but Dad refused for us to go to church because he was not allowed to be a full member. Mum and Dad were unable to receive the Sacrament of Holy Communion and their civil marriage was not recognised.

'We must take the children to church, Ben,' Mum would plead. 'We can't let them grow up not practising their faith.'

Dad was adamant that if he could not partake in the Sacraments, then neither he nor we would set foot inside the church again.

Mum later started taking us to the Dutch Reformed Church at the end of our street. This infuriated Dad even more because this church was the foundation of the racist Afrikaner community. It supported the government's system of apartheid and their churches in white areas were clearly marked for their use only. The church service was formal and everything was in proper Afrikaans, which we found hard to understand.

Sometimes, on special occasions, we attended St Anne's Catholic Church with Mum's close friend Sally Hanniball and her family. Mrs Hanniball grew up close to where Mum lived and had attended the same primary school. A tall dark woman, Mrs Hanniball often visited our house to seek Mum's counsel. Mr Hanniball was a bus driver and they had four children, including twins whom they called Girlie and Boy. It was years later that I found out their names actually were Hilda and Hilton.

To help make ends meet Mum tried her hand at anything. When she was not busy cooking or cleaning, she would be sewing or knitting and selling the products to the neighbours. Sometimes she would exchange her knitting for a chicken or some eggs from Mrs Africa across the road.

Mum saved money by turning the worn collars on Dad's shirts inside out to make them look new again. She would unpick his old trousers to make shorts for Georgie and Owen, and skirts or pinafores for us. Old double bed sheets were cut in half to make single bed sheets and pillow cases by carefully cutting away the worn parts; the discarded bits were used for floor rags. Old towels were cut into squares to use as hand towels or facecloths. Old dresses were redesigned into clothes for us. Using her knowledge of embroidery, she created smocked dresses and knitted lacy socks with a special cotton. Discarded pieces of fabric were cut into ribbons for our hair. Remnant pieces of flannelette were made into pyjamas.

For special occasions like Sundays or Christmas, Mum would buy a chicken from Mrs Africa to roast for lunch. On our first Christmas Eve in Chimes Street, I followed Georgie across the road.

'Why are we going to Mrs Africa?' I asked.

'Mum said that I must collect a chicken,' Georgie replied.

Mrs Africa's house was always busy. Neighbours went there to buy eggs, chickens and vegetables. We would see them leave carrying parcels wrapped in newspaper or brown paper bags.

'Just wait here in the kitchen,' said Johnny, Mrs Africa's son.

Disappearing through the horizontally divided backdoor, Johnny closed the bottom half leaving the top half open. Peeking over the door along the fence, we saw the yard was filled with timber and wire mesh-covered pens. The chickens flapped around wildly as Mrs Africa closed the wire mesh gate behind her.

Johnny slipped back in and thrust a tiny chick into my hand. Touching the soft fur, the chick squeaked and wriggled around. Reluctantly, I handed the soft furry chick back to Johnny.

Over the door opening we watched Mrs Africa climb over the wire mesh with a big chicken tucked under her arm. The chicken flapped and squealed as she headed for the wooden stump in the corner. With one hand holding the chicken down, she reached with her free hand for the handle of the chopper.

Spotting us at the door, she shouted, 'Johnny, close the door; let the children wait in the kitchen.'

From behind the closed door we heard a loud thump and a squealing sound.

'That chicken is running around with an off-head,' laughed Johnny, running around the table flapping his head.

I rubbed my neck and turned my head from side to side. *How could a chicken run around the backyard without a head?* I looked at Georgie, his face was pale and he stared at the wall.

'Flap, flap,' laughed Johnny. 'That chicken is dead.'

Mrs Africa walked into the kitchen with a parcel wrapped in newspaper. On one side it was soaked in blood. She placed it inside a brown paper bag, then wiped her hands before handing it to Georgie.

'Tell your mummy to return my bowl,' she said as she handed me a small bowl filled with eggs, little feathers still stuck on them.

Georgie held his arm outstretched to the side keeping the bag away from his body. As we walked across the road, my eyes remained fixed on the bag, watching for any movement that might indicate the headless chicken was still alive.

'Put the bag on the sink,' Mum told Georgie as we walked through the front door. Georgie pushed the brown paper bag away from him and wiped his hand on the cloth. He disappeared while Frances and I watched Mum unwrap the parcel. The chicken lay lifeless on its side, the neck in place but the head missing. Mum worked quietly, plucking the feathers, cutting off the feet, then holding the pale body under the running tap. Frances picked up a feather from the ground and put it in her pocket.

That Christmas lunch, Georgie and I sat staring at the roast chicken on the table.

'Eat your food,' Mum pleaded, but Georgie refused to eat the chicken even when Mum promised him the wishbone.

Dad came home from work that Christmas evening with plates of food and presents from people at the hotel. A doll with blond hair and bright red lips for me, a pretty dress for Maureen, a small car for Owen, a book for Frances, and a bat and ball for Georgie.

That evening, we heard Mum and Dad talking about us going with Mr and Mrs Hanniball on a bus to the church picnic.

'I can leave Maureen with Mrs Khune,' Mum said. 'Sally and Hilton have invited us to come along to the picnic for the day.'

'I don't want to have anything to do with the church,' Dad said.

'It's just a picnic, Ben. In this hot weather, the children will be able to play in the dam with all the other children.'

3

OWEN'S STAR

**DARLING, SOUTH AFRICA: JANUARY 1962,
MID-SUMMER**

Too excited to sleep, we rose early on Sunday morning ready for our first family picnic. Dad stayed behind because he had to work. Frances and Georgie were already dressed and ready to go long before we had to leave. Mum was busy in the kitchen preparing sandwiches, packing them in the round metal tin with the kitten on the lid. On the sink, in a bowl of cold water, the boiled eggs were cooling, and a brown paper bag filled with apples and oranges stood on the kitchen table. The armchair was filled with a bag of clothes, towels, blankets and pillows.

'Dress yourselves and come and eat your porridge,' called Mum as she busied herself packing the food.

Mum had sewed green bathers for Owen and me. Frances helped the two of us get dressed. She pulled my hair into a ponytail and plaited my long hair while I ate my porridge.

'Sit still and eat your porridge otherwise we will be late for the bus,' Mum told Georgie who was bouncing up and down in his chair.

Owen sat quietly at the dining room table eating his porridge, dressed in white shorts and a shirt over his bather. His curly hair neatly combed.

Mum carried on packing the food, singing softly to herself, *'Jesus loves me this I know, for the Bible tells me so.'*

Mrs Khune called 'Good morning,' as she walked through the front door. Patting Owen on his head, she placed a small cake tin next to the fruit on the table.

'I made these biscuits for the children,' she said, picking Maureen up and reaching for her bag of clothes. 'Enjoy the picnic, and Frances, look after your brothers and sister.' She was smiling at us as she turned to walk back to her house with Maureen.

At last it was time to walk down the road to the bus. Dad was asleep in the bedroom and we left without saying goodbye. If only Dad knew then that this day would change his life forever.

Georgie, heavily laden carrying a tin filled with sandwiches in one hand and a bag of fruit in the other, walked ahead of us. I had two pillows tucked under my arms and Frances carried the blankets. Mum carried the bag with extra clothes and held Owen's hand.

Mr and Mrs Khune stood at the gate waving. The bus was parked on the corner where Mr and Mrs Hanniball and three of their children, Fransie and the twins Girlie and Boy, along with many other people were waiting to board.

Once the bus started to move, the noisy engine and swaying made me feel sick. Mum gave me an orange to suck and I laid with my head in Frances's lap. Mum, with Owen sleeping in her lap, sat with Mrs Hanniball in the seat behind.

The excited voices of the children getting off the bus woke me. We had arrived in Darling, a small town in a farming community about 75 kilometres from Cape Town. The picnic spot, filled with trees and patches of grass, reminded me of the pictures in my story books.

'There is the dam,' one of the boys yelled out as he pointed. 'It's behind the trees, come and see.'

The sunlight danced on the water; it was the very first time that we could walk and splash about in a dam. We had never been to the beach and could not swim.

While the men set up the picnic spot we raced each other to see who could take off our clothes the fastest before running straight into the dam, shrieking and splashing about. So much fun we had frolicking in the water under the blazing sun. Near the edge, in the cool shallow water, the watermelon lay anchored in the sand.

Frances, Georgie and the older children could walk deeper into the dam. Girlie, Boy and I, who were the same height, followed them as far as we could until the water reached to our necks. In some parts, we walked on our toes to keep our heads above the water.

'Gather the children for some watermelon,' someone shouted.

Drying ourselves in the sun, we heard Mum call out, 'Owen! Owen, where are you?'

One of the children said that Owen had wandered into the bush to pick berries. Frances cuddled Georgie and me while Mum frantically ran around, ducking between the bushes. The adults formed a search party and spread around calling out his name.

'Owen, Owen!' Mum's voice echoed over the open space.

Mr Hanniball and another man waded through the dam, the water lapped at their knees. They stopped, knelt, and slowly lifted something out of the water.

My arm dangled down the side of my body, the slice of watermelon in my hand felt heavy and cold. Frances drew me closer as she patted my shoulder and touched my wet hair. The man laid Owen on the grass. I waited for him to move his head and open his eyes. People were shouting and some women wailed.

'Eat your watermelon,' Frances whispered in my ear.

'Sarah, Sarah, they found Owen,' Mrs Hanniball cried out as the men lay him on the ground.

Owen didn't move. His face had a shade of blue and wet tangled curls clung to his forehead.

Water dripped down my back and front, splashing onto my feet. My fingers stiffened. The watermelon dropped to the ground. I turned to look for Mum and saw her running towards us.

Mr Hanniball knelt over Owen, the other man started blowing into his mouth and pushing on his stomach. Water trickled down the side of Owen's mouth as the man continued to grip and squeeze his little body. His eyelids gently covered his green eyes.

Mum's voice echoed through the bushes. Holding her face in her hands, she threw herself on the ground next to Owen. Sobbing hysterically, Mum touched Owen's body as the men tried to revive him. Some of the ladies were crying and holding Mum as she called out his name. The man stopped blowing in Owen's mouth, touched his hair, then gently ran his hand over his face.

Turning to Mum, his head down cast, he said, 'Sorry, Mrs Crosher, Owen is dead.'

Shaking her head, Mum cried out, 'No. No. No, he is not dead. Please try again and blow into his mouth.'

Mr Hanniball put his arm around Mum and said softly, 'Sarah, I am sorry, he is dead. He swallowed too much water.'

Cradling Owen in her arms, Mum cried as she rocked him, talking to him, willing him to wake up. Frances held her arms tightly around me. Tears trickled down her face.

'He swallowed a lot of water and it's coming out of his mouth,' Georgie whispered.

Chaos ensued as people hurriedly gathered their children and belongings. Frances quickly dried me before putting on my clothes. Squeezing the water out of my hair she gathered it in a ponytail. Georgie was already dressed.

Mum was still sitting on the ground rocking Owen in her arms. He looked like he was asleep. I wanted to touch him, to wake him, but Mum had wrapped him tightly in a blanket. The noise of the bus engine filled the air. Gathering our wet towels, Frances took my hand and called Georgie to follow Mum as she walked towards the bus.

On the back seat, we sat closely together on either side of Mum. Her eyes were fixed on Owen. Only the sound of the engine was audible as the bus made its way back. Some children turned to look back at us as we drove along the long road home.

We stopped at a police station near Darling, where

Mum had to report Owen's death and get a death certificate before we could take his body home.

'No, I will carry him,' Mum said refusing Mr Hanniball's help as she walked down the aisle and the steps towards the police station.

After a while, the bus started up and I saw Mum walking towards us. An uneasy silence hung over the bus. The jubilant sound of the children on our way to the picnic spot now replaced by confused expressions.

It was after sunset when the bus finally manoeuvred its way down our narrow street. Our house lights were switched on and Dad stood waiting in the doorway. Mr Hanniball walked in front holding Owen's wrapped body above his head. We followed Mum to the front door.

'No. No,' I heard Dad scream. 'Not my boy. My boy, my baby boy.'

Mrs Khune stood at the door holding Maureen in her arms. Dad's screams continued. I looked at him laying on the floor with Owen next to him still wrapped in the blanket.

Mum sobbed, 'Ben, I am sorry, I thought he was playing with the children, I looked for him in the bushes,' she tried to explain, the words tumbling out, not making any sense.

Dad lay on the floor.

Mr Khune sat down next to him, quietly saying, 'Come, Mr Crosher, you must get up, Owen can't lay on the ground. We must lay his body on a table. I will help you to do it.'

Pulling Dad up into a sitting position, Mr Khune placed Owen in his arms. We sat next to Mum on the floor, watching Dad cradle Owen. Dad's tears dropping on Owen's face. I stared at Owen's face, his eyes closed, his body limp. I wanted him to sit up and smile the way he always did. But, he looked as if he was asleep.

The neighbours had gathered and as the news spread, more and more people stood outside the door, spilling into the street. Mrs Africa came rushing in from across the road and Mum collapsed in her arms. She sat comforting Mum as she wept. Mrs Africa soon started waving people away from the door.

For the next few hours the house was busy. Mrs Africa and Mum worked quietly setting up the bed with the piece of wood and a sink sheet Mr Khune carried over. They placed the sink sheet on two chairs to form a bed and put a blanket at the bottom, covered with a white sheet.

Placing Owen's body on the bed, Dad leaned over him, stroking his hair as his tears fell. Mr Khune brought flowers from his garden and placed them around Owen's face. Mum covered him with another sheet and Mrs Africa put some candles in glass jars and lit them around his face.

That night we slept in our bed next to Owen. The flickering candles cast shadows on the walls. Mum moved about the house quietly, never far from Owen, wiping his face and body with oil and keeping the candles burning. During the day, his face was open and surrounded by flowers; at night it was covered with a sheet. His light-brown curly hair was combed with a curl in the front.

The house had a strong smell of flowers mixed with the sweet scent of the oils Mum used to put on Owen's face. Family and neighbours visited and brought food for us to eat and more flowers to put next to Owen. People spoke softly when they were around Owen, as if he could hear them.

'He looks like an angel. He looks so peaceful,' they sympathised with Mum.

Mrs Khune was a great comfort to Mum and to us. She changed into black clothing and quietly fed and bathed us and helped serve tea when visitors arrived. The next morning Mr Hanniball took Dad to arrange the funeral.

Owen was buried three days later, dressed in a white gown, his face surrounded with flowers in a small white coffin.

On the day of the funeral, the neighbours lined the streets as the funeral cars drove down Chimes Street to the Catholic church. Dad wept as he entered the church with Mr Hanniball helping him to carry the coffin.

'Mr Crosher, I am sorry about your son's death,' the priest said. 'I will come and see you next week, and you and your family must come back to the church.'

I missed Owen, his smiling face, the way he followed me around the house, and the two of us sitting at the table having our meals while Frances and Georgie went to school.

In the days and weeks that followed Mum busied herself with cleaning the house and sewing for the Dutch Reformed Church bazaar. The scent of flowers mixed with sweet oils hung around the lounge room where we slept; for many years it reminded me of Owen. I felt him around me whenever I smelt flowers, as if he were following me.

A few Saturdays after Owen was buried we took the bus to the cemetery with flowers, carrying a bucket and

Mr Khune's garden tools. We sat around the grave, cleaning it up, wetting the sand and building a round mound in the shape of the coffin. Mr Khune made a white cross with the name Owen painted on it to mark his grave.

One day, we stopped going, because Mum said that it cost too much money for us all to travel on the bus. Mum never talked about Owen. It was as if he was never in the house.

Mr Hanniball had taken a group photograph of us at the picnic. It was blurry but he managed to capture Owen's face out of the group. That was the only photograph we had of Owen. His light-brown curls gleamed in the sun; dressed in his green bathing suit, his face looked sad. The framed photo stood on our half-moon table next to a small vase filled with flowers. I felt Owen's eyes on me as I played in the lounge room or sat at the table.

In the evening, whenever we sat on the hill, Mrs Khune would point at the sky searching for Owen's star.

'When you look up at the stars, look for one that is flickering and you will know, that is Owen,' she said.

In the weeks after he died we would climb to the top of the hill to search the sky, hoping to be the first to spot his flickering star. One of us would point out a flickering star, convinced that we were the first to see Owen's star.

Two weeks after Owen died, I started school at Steenberg No. 2 Primary where Frances was in Grade 4 and George in Grade 3. My teacher, Mrs Williams, was friendly, with short, curly dark hair.

'Your little brother is in heaven,' she told me on my first day. 'This table and chair is yours,' she said, and pointing to a book and pen on my table, she added, 'And, this is your writing book and that is your pencil.'

Mrs Williams paid extra attention to me, always smiling and making sure that I was playing with the other children during play-time or sitting next to someone at our little tables during class. I loved school and my first reading book was 'Sus en Daan', a colourful illustrated children's book

Their adventures in the forest reminded me of playing in the sand hills at the back of our house. I was fascinated with the stories of the animals, and looked forward to story-time to hear more about Sus and Daan climbing trees, their monkey Kees, the bird, Koeloe the turkey, and the donkey. Whenever it was reading time, Mrs Williams gently coaxed me to join in repeating the words she read out, 'Sus en Daan is maats' ('Maats means 'friends')

'Sus en Daan is maats,' we repeated in unison.

When Mum fetched me from school she'd spend a few minutes talking to Mrs Williams before we walked home, with Mum pushing Maureen in the pram.

Steenberg, South Africa: January 1963, Summer

Mum's belly had been growing bigger over the cooler months. She spent her time knitting and making baby clothes. Early one morning, we woke up to moaning sounds coming from Mum's bedroom. Through the crack in the door we saw Mrs Africa wiping Mum's face. In a soothing voice she whispered, 'Nurse Wichtman is on her way.'

Mrs Khune took us next door to play and we climbed to the top of the hill. There we sat watching as Nurse Wichtman cycled up the road with her small black case strapped to the back of her bicycle. Our eyes searched the mountains in the distance for the spot where Mrs Khune said babies came from. The familiar black taxi drove up our street to collect Dad for work.

Before getting in, as he always did, he took out a cloth, wiped his shoes and stopped to wave.

'You have a new brother,' Dad said, and then got into the taxi.

When the nurse left, we went into Mum's room and stood around the bed. The baby, with a chubby face and thick black curly hair, lay in Mum's arms.

'This is your new brother. His name is Andrew but we will call him Andy.' Mum looked tired but smiled and let us look at the baby wrapped in a yellow blanket.

Mrs Khune always came around to take Maureen next door while Mum recovered.

'Andy is a big baby and you must rest, Mrs Crosher,' she said. 'I will look after the children and bring some food over.'

On windy days, when the sand blew from the hills onto the street, the hawkers struggled through the thick sand with their horse-drawn carts filled with fruit, vegetables or fish. Whenever we heard the wailing of the fish horn we would run outside to look at bunches of fish covered with wet sacks on the back of the cart. Sometimes Mrs Africa would exchange eggs for a bunch of fish and would give Mum one for our dinner. That night we'd have fish cakes made with parsley from Mr Khune's garden and mashed potato with a tomato smoortjie: a sauce made with onions and tomatoes.

During those months, after Andy was born, Mum sewed clothes for the church bazaar. The lounge room was filled with boxes of fabric and Mum's sewing basket filled with cotton.

When Mrs Demes from the council office called to collect the weekly rent, she saw the material laid out on the table.

'Can I buy some of the material?'

Mum and Mrs Demes had attended primary school together. They talked about family and friends whom they both knew, and of their school days.

'As soon as the baby is a bit older I am going to look for work,' Mum said.

As Mrs Demes looked around our cramped space, she said, 'There's a bigger house not far from here where someone is moving out. It has two bedrooms and a big backyard. I will let you know next week when the house will be available.'

'Take some material,' Mum said happily to Mrs Demes, showing her a few pieces of material.

4

DIVISION

A few weeks later, on a Tuesday, Mum was up early, packing the last of our belongings for our move to Pickerill Street.

'We'll come back and visit,' Mum said to Mrs Khune. 'Once the house is straight you must come and visit us.'

Mrs Khune nodded, dabbing her eyes as she smiled and waved, hugging Maureen one last time before putting her on the side bar.

'Hold on tightly,' she said, smiling through her tears. 'Goodbye children, look after each other and come back to visit us.'

I looked at the hills behind our house. They held so many of our childhood memories. We were leaving behind the vast playground—our sacred spot where we dug holes and buried our treasures.

The hills, the place where we hid our fears and sang our happy songs, was our solace. It echoed with laughter as we raced each other down the hill on sink sleds. The rolling hills captured the pulse of our racing hearts as we hid from each other in our caves; or heard our shrieks at finding a bush of juicy red berries, and kept secret our visits to the forbidden sand dunes further back. They sapped our energy, leaving us exhausted at night as we washed the sand off our weary bodies.

As we walked down the street I turned back to look at the house. Mr Khune stood behind the gate, his hat lowered over his face. Johnny stood next to Mrs Africa, waving from across the road. At the corner, I turned to look back once more. Mr Khune had his arm around Mrs Khune, they were still waving.

Mum walked in silence, looking straight ahead as she pushed the heavily laden pram through the sand-filled road. She was leaving behind a place holding her own memories of heartache and sadness. Owen's memory the saddest of all.

In September 1963, the move into Pickerill Street was life-changing for our family. We had our own bedroom again and Mum could open the windows and doors every morning to air the house. Our school, now renamed Harmony Primary, was across the road—the gates locked for the holidays.

Our house, a semi-detached, was the second last house in the street. The front fence, covered by an overgrown hedge, had a small opening for the gate and along the side a wider opening leading to the wire fenced backyard.

From the front windows we had a view of the False Bay Mountain Ranges stretching from one end of our sight-line across to where it disappeared in the distance. In the summer sunlight, the mountains appeared light blue and when the sun set behind it, the skyline would be ablaze in orange and red. During the cold winter months, the clouds and mist poured over the peaks, leaving the skies grey and dark.

Mum took great delight in decorating the home. The kitchen had bright yellow handmade curtains and the old wooden table was covered in a matching tablecloth, neatly stitched with embroidered edges. The green Jewel wood-fired stove took up a lot of space but kept the house cosy and warm during the winter months.

'This house is bigger and brighter than the other house and the backyard is big enough for us to grow our own vegetables. We can live here forever,' she would often remark, as if she wanted to wipe the other house from her memory.

In the lounge room, across from the front door, hung a familiar photo frame—the red glowing Sacred Heart of Jesus. Tucked in the corner of the frame was the small blurry photograph of Owen taken shortly before he drowned.

On the half-moon table stood the same framed photograph of Owen. In the silence, I could hear Owen's laughter, his little voice ringing in my ears, calling out to us as we played hide and seek.

Next door lived Mr and Mrs Hendricks with their nine children—four sons and five daughters—crammed into a two-bedroomed house. Mr Hendricks, a war veteran, had an eye injury. When he was drunk he yelled at his family, sending them screaming and running into the backyard or out on the street.

Mrs Hendricks, a sweet and gentle soul who hardly ever ventured out of the house, bore the brunt of his rantings. We could hear her sewing machine in our lounge room as she worked for many hours, day and night, making clothes and doing alterations for neighbours.

On the other side, in another two-bedroomed semi-detached, lived Mr and Mrs Oliver and their six daughters and one son. Mrs Oliver's younger sister also lived with them. Mrs Oliver, with her smiling face and welcoming manner, knew everyone in the area and kept a watchful eye over the neighbourhood children. The Olivers had been moved under the Group Areas Act from an area near Bo-Kaap, on the slopes of Signal Hill, a mountain near the city centre.

Mrs Oliver cooked delicious Malay-style curries with aromas and spices new to us. Most days, as she went about cooking or cleaning, we could hear her soothing voice singing her favourite songs. When Mr Oliver was home he would harmonise with her. Often they sang a duet called *Hey Paula,* which was popular at the time.

Mrs Oliver, who loved beautiful things, always had a stream of salesman knocking on her door, selling merchandise or collecting payments. She took pride in displaying her household items and had great taste in decorating her home. On laundry day, her washing lines, raised by the longest poles, displayed sparkling white linen and rows of underwear as they flapped in the breeze.

The women used a mysterious little blue square stone in the final rinse water to make the white garments sparkling bright. Bluesil, as it was referred to, was a fine blue iron powder wrapped in a piece of cloth to prevent the residue from spreading directly onto the laundry.

'You need only three pairs of panties and vests: one for the body, one for the drawer and one in the wash,'

Mum would say. 'When you finish your studies, you will get good jobs, earn high wages—and then you will be able to buy many beautiful things.'

'Don't worry Mum, when I start working I will buy you a robot to do all the cleaning,' quipped Georgie.

Our housing estate, like many spread along the area called the Cape Flats, was home to families classified as coloured. As a result of Mum and Dad's mixed heritage, my siblings and I were classified at birth as coloured. Families in our neighbourhood had been uprooted from their homes in areas declared for white people under the government's Group Areas Act of 1950.

Our neighbours came from areas such as Constantia, Newlands, Harfield, Simonstown, Diep River, Steurhof and Bo-Kaap. Many spoke about their struggle with displacement, the pain of losing their homes, and they mourned the separation of families.

The government's carefully crafted plan created cities for white people and townships for non-whites. Only the best and most scenic areas were allocated to white people. Prime areas, with pristine beaches, sea views or near the foot of the mountains, were rezoned to make them exclusively white.

Coloured people were moved to what was known as the Cape Flats. This was mostly confined to flood-prone areas and to the sand hills. Indian people, who accounted for a small percentage of the Cape population, were moved to their designated area, called Rylands.

Black men in the Cape, stripped of their rights to live as ordinary citizens, were herded into townships and their families moved to the independent homeland in Transkei. The government passed a law that those who could obtain a work permit in the Cape had to carry a pass identification book.

One of Mum's friends, Frans—he worked as a kitchen hand at the Marina Hotel in Muizenberg— was classified as black and forced into the black township.

Frans had lived with his family in Vryground, a short distance from his work place Now he had to move to the township of Gugulethu, a long distance away. His wife, a teacher at a school in the township, made it possible for them to stay together as a family.

Under the Group Areas Act the government had the power to racially segregate its citizens into four groups—Native (Nguni-speaking blacks), White, Indian and Coloured—to prevent inter-racial contact, particularly socially and through marriage.

The Act gave most white citizens exclusive rights and privileges to own prime property and the best facilities to enrich their lives.

The government's master plan was to move those whom they classified as non-whites to areas away from the city with inadequate services.

Many men in the community had been deployed to North Africa and some to Italy during World War II. They were the owners of black bicycles. At the end of the war, white soldiers were continued on full army pay while coloureds were 'rewarded' with black bicycles. Black soldiers were discharged without compensation.

Like Mr Khune, not many spoke about the horrors of war. Those who had tales to tell spoke about being assigned firstly to guarding duties without guns. When the Italian army arrived in Kenya, soldiers like one of my uncles, who had received limited training, were only then issued with guns to join the forces, black and white on the front-line.

The psychological trauma of war, coupled with displacement under apartheid, resulted in excessive use of alcohol among many in our neighbourhood. This was one of the main contributing factors for the high rate of domestic abuse.

Domestic violence was evident in our community. The women often hid their blackened eyes behind dark glasses, or hid bruises to their necks and faces with scarves. They formed little groups to counsel and support each other through those hard times. Saturday nights, with their husbands drunk and asleep early, they would go out dancing at the local Retreat Hotel. For a few hours, their struggles forgotten.

With limited means of supporting themselves because of family responsibilities, many women felt trapped and vulnerable. They often sought Mum's counsel and support. Despite her own difficulties, Mum listened and advised many women on how to improve their lives. Her advice centred on women developing a survival mentality through creating a happy home environment, living within their means and pushing for their children to be educated.

Fortunately, in our home, Dad was no match for Mum's strong and determined character. She made no distinction between Georgie, Frances and me in terms of responsibilities like cleaning the yard or washing dishes. She strongly enforced the rule that we all take responsibility for keeping the house tidy.

Georgie and I loved exploring our new neighbourhood. Our backyard, filled with patches of grass, spilled onto an open field with scattered sunflowers and small bushes leading to a sports field. A shallow ravine ran down the side of the neighbour's house until it disappeared underground near the sports field at the back of our yard.

All the streets in the area had musical names. Pickerill Street, a cul-de-sac, ended at the ravine. On the other side stretched a vast area of bushland: an area Mum had forbidden us from entering because it looked unsafe.

'This street is named after William Pickerill, the former musical director of the Municipal Symphony Orchestra,' Dad explained. 'Mr Pickerill was known to have resurrected the orchestra and kept it going during the war, and the council honoured him by giving musical names to all the streets in Steenberg.'

The ravine was the gathering point for children in the neighbourhood where we played games and slid across the narrow pole to the other side. Georgie was eager to test his skills at walking across the narrow two-metre long pipe. The first time he tried he landed in the water below. The children gasped, then laughed as he pulled himself back up, dripping wet—only to try again, this time turning back when he started to wobble.

That moment brought an acceptance of us into the neighbourhood. The children's laughter echoed across the open space as Georgie continued his attempts to walk the pipe. Here I met Cheryl, who became my best friend. Her family lived in the other semi-detached next door.

I recognised Cheryl from school but we had never played together. She had long light-brown hair tied in a ponytail, and her green eyes lit up her pale skin. She, like me, was the middle child in her family.

'I miss our house in Bo-Kaap, near the mountains,' she told me. 'Some of my friends still live there. My older sister Jenny still lives there with our grandmother. We only see Jenny during the school holidays. But soon she will come home because my grandmother must also move. I have a Muslim name too: it's Arsia. Our neighbours in the Bo-Kaap gave me that name.'

The many different cultural influences enriched our neighbourhood, spilling out onto our streets and breathing life into our surroundings. Summer evenings, we would walk around our streets looking at the beautiful gardens. People took pride in their homes, many painting the top half of their homes and laying concrete paths up to the gate. Easter, Christmas and Eid were the most magical time. It was a time of celebration and inclusion.

At Easter, pickled fish and hot cross buns were the traditional fare to feed us on Good Friday. Pickled fish (also known as *Ingelegde Vis*) is Cape Town's soul food; it combines Asian, African and European elements. There are so many stories about the origins of pickled fish. Stories such as an abundance of fish or the belief that women should not cook on Good Friday are among the folklore. The fried fish, preferably snoek or yellowtail marinated in vinegar and flavoured with curried onions, became popular as a method to preserve fish.

Around the corner in Solo Street lived Mr and Mrs Jeptha, a Muslim family, who introduced us to syrup-dipped and coconut-sprinkled doughnuts called koeksisters (or 'koesiestas', as we used to say), flaky roti, hot and spicy curries, samosas and a variety of cookies. Mrs Jeptha, a soft-spoken woman, was always busy cooking and looking after her own children as well as those of her extended family.

During Ramadan, just before sunset, we would eagerly wait for the Jeptha boys to deliver small plates of *koesiestas*, spicy hot daaltjies (chilli bites) and sweet pumpkin fritters. The boys, washed and neatly dressed, wearing white crochet skull caps, would walk around our street delivering the eats before disappearing indoors to break the fast.

Mrs Jeptha's house would burst at the seams with family and friends as they celebrated Eid al-fitr, the end of Ramadan, or Labarang, as the local Muslims call it. Knowing that they would serve everyone plates of food, cakes and sweets, we would play in the street in front of their door until they called us inside.

The children, dressed in new clothes and shoes, with the boys wearing their distinctive red koffiahs, would walk around the neighbourhood knocking on doors. 'Slamat for Labarang,' they would greet, waiting for coins to be dropped in their hands before going to the next house.

It was a joyous time and all of us joined in the celebrations, walking behind them in the streets or listening to the men's choir singing in Mrs Jeptha's backyard.

Rampies Sny, a Cape Malay tradition commemorating the birth of Prophet Muhammed, was another special event. During January Muslim women and girls, wearing pretty dresses, would participate in the cultural Rampies Cutting Ceremony. Women gathered at the mosque to cut lemon leaves on cutting boards, then mixed them with orange oil before sprinkling the offering with rosewater. To increase the aroma, they would burn frankincense below the tray of leaves while praying for blessings.

The leaves would then be packaged in sachets and left in the mosque for the men as gifts. Receiving one of the sachets was a privilege and one that I treasured.

The Meintjies family in our neighbourhood owned a fridge and a car. They sold red and green toffee apples and syrup-flavoured ice blocks. On hot summer days, Georgie and I would join the queue at their gate to buy two ice blocks for a cent. The best part was sucking the sweet syrupy flavour that left orange, red or green stains on our lips and tongues, then letting the ice freeze the tips of our tongues.

Frances, who was now 11 and in her last year in primary school, was always helping Mum with housework and taking care of Maureen and Andy. She missed out on these special treats and getting to know the people in the neighbourhood. She struggled with her thick frizzy hair and spent many hours in rollers to tame her unruly hair.

The only time she ventured out was to call us to come home or to go to the shop. She took her responsibility of caring for us after school very seriously and her sudden appearance and the tone in her voice would signal the urgency for us to go home.

Shortly after moving into Pickerill Street we had a surprise visit from Mr and Mrs Khune. They arrived bearing a tin of biscuits and some fruit. Mrs Khune scooped Maureen into her arms and hugged her tightly. We huddled around Mr Khune to look at the contents of the shoe box in his hand. The lid had several holes and inside, nestled on a bed of mulberry leaves, six silkworms crawled around. Smiling broadly, Frances gently moved the leaves around to expose the silkworms. Listening intently to

Mr Khune's instructions, she immediately took on the responsibility of caring for our new pets.

Mr and Mrs Khune slowly faded from our lives.

A few weeks later, Mum announced that she had found a job at Kleyweg, a Dutch bakery near Muizenberg along the False Bay coastline. The Dutch owners, Mr and Mrs Kleyweg, supplied businesses with their pastries and catered for functions.

'It will take me about an hour to get to work by bicycle,' Mum explained.

'Who will take care of Andy while we are at school,' I asked Frances.

'Don't worry,' she reassured me. 'Mum will find someone to stay here during the day until I get home from school.'

Before she started work, Mum introduced us to Rosie, a young girl who lived in Vrygrond. She would take care of us while Mum was at work. Rosie, who hardly spoke to us, preferred to sit in the sun with rollers in her hair, smoking and reading magazines. Uninterested in us, she was always in front of the mirror, applying make-up or standing at the front gate. As soon as Frances arrived home from school, Rosie would take off her pink housecoat, remove the rollers to style her hair, then put on high heel shoes and red lipstick before leaving.

One morning, when I was home sick from school, Rosie waited until Frances and Georgie had left for school. 'Get up, we are going for a walk down the road,' she said.

Pushing Andy in the pram, Maureen and I followed her down the street, then turned into Viola Street, along Sibelius Avenue into Symphony Avenue, then along

Orchestra Street, turning into Military Road towards the bushland on the other side of Prince George Drive.

'Where are we going Rosie?' I asked. Without looking back, she replied, 'To my mother's house.'

After we crossed Prince George Drive, she pulled the pram along the sand-filled paths between the small wood and iron shacks and headed to a house close to the bushes. Walking through the black sand between the shacks, people sat around outside the shacks smoking and talking. My eyes fearfully scanned the area.

Holding the pram with her one hand she opened the door and pushed the pram inside leaving the door slightly ajar. There were no windows and only a ray of light beamed through the door opening. Squinting my eyes, trying to adjust to the dim light, I sat down on a box against the wall.

'It will get light now, now,' she said softly, as if she didn't want anyone else to hear.

'Why do you have newspapers on the walls?' I asked.

'That's to keep the place warm,' she said as she sat Maureen down on the chair next to the table. Andy lay asleep in the pram.

'I am coming now, now,' she said before disappearing through the doorway.

I sat looking at the newspapers on the wall, then I heard loud screams coming from outside. Moving closer to the door opening, I could see people gathered around a girl rolling on the ground. With her arm outstretched, as if she wanted to grab hold of something, she moaned, 'Help me, help me'. Someone poured water on her face, making her squirm and wriggle away. In a hoarse voice she continued to cry out, 'Please, help me,' as a man in the crowd prodded her with a stick.

'She is bewitched, don't touch her,' the man told the crowd. 'I saw the Tokoloshe next to her bed. Then he ran out of the house into the bushes; he was this high,' he continued, measuring his hand to his hip. Lowering his voice, he turned his head in the direction of the bushes, and whispered, 'He had big ears and a green cap on his head.'

The women held each other, shaking their heads and looked in the direction of the bushes.

'Yes, the Tokoloshe is a dwarf and he has been running around here at night getting up to no good,' one lady said.

The girl's body jerked. Waving her arms wildly, she tried again to grab something in the air as white foamy saliva trickled down the side of her mouth.

Scared and shaken, my eyes scanned the room searching for the Tokoloshe. Panicked, I started crying, lifted Maureen off the chair and grabbed hold of the pram. With one hand pushing Andy in the pram and holding on to Maureen's hand with the other, I walked into the sunlight.

'Rosie, Rosie,' I whimpered, while tears streamed down my face. Squinting in the sunlight, I saw Rosie running out of another house towards us. Hastily she straightened her clothes and smoothed her hair. Grabbing hold of the pram she rushed past the crowd. I took Maureen's hand and ran behind her.

That evening, as darkness settled, I sat in Mum's room, fearful of the Tokoloshe. Sensing my unease, Mum asked, 'What's wrong, child?'

Tears streamed down my face and through my sobs, I asked, 'Can Mummy put bricks under the beds to make it higher.'

'Why, what's wrong?' she coaxed, gently wiping my tears.

'There was a *Tokeloshie* at Rosie's house and he saw me. He will find us in the night and come to our bed,' I sobbed.

In between sobs I told Mum the whole story.

Cradling me in her arms she said reassuringly, 'There is no such thing as a Tokoloshe. It's a made-up story that people believe in and they use it to scare each other with.'

The next morning when Rosie arrived, Mum sent her away and by the next day she had found an older lady to take care of us during the school term.

We continued living blissfully happy in Pickerill Street. Georgie and I had made many friends that summer. Friday afternoons we would help Frances polish the floors with Cobra, a lavender-scented wax. Georgie quickly worked out a way to make it easier to shine it up. With my feet firmly on the cloth, he would pull me along the passage and around the furniture in the rooms, leaving a shiny trail.

Saturday mornings we'd take turns to trample blankets in the aluminium bath after they had been soaked for a few hours. Between the three of us, we'd wring out as much water as we could by gripping the blanket at either end, twisting and turning it, before hanging it out to dry.

Frances, always the supervisor, kept the house spotless until Mum returned in the evening. She was also in charge of warming the food once Georgie had lit the stove. The three of us, with differing personalities, clashed many times, but our bond as siblings always won out in the end. Georgie continued a power struggle with Frances and often resented that she had been born first.

Georgie, in a hurry to get back out to play, was often

the cause of the many arguments between him and Frances. This left me wandering around on my own or seeking Maureen's and Andy's company.

STEENBERG, SOUTH AFRICA: JANUARY 1965, MID-SUMMER

During the school holidays, we woke up to the droning of machinery. It came from behind the bushes on the other side of the ravine. Cheryl and other neighbourhood children had gathered at the ravine but Georgie was the first to explore the mystery sound behind the bushes.

Taking it in turns to cross the ravine, by sliding across the pipe, we crept into the bushes closer to where the noise was coming from. To our astonishment, a large area had been cleared, trees and bushes laid in piles and workmen were loading the vegetation onto trucks. Two tractors moved up and down, leaving wide tracks and flattening anything in sight.

As we crossed the open space, we saw a few houses closer to the railway line. In the distance, for the first time, I saw a train pass by and on the other side of the track we could see bigger houses.

Little did I know that on the other side of the railway line, children were leading privileged lives.

That summer, a triple tragedy struck our peaceful neighbourhood. During one of our expeditions across the ravine to where the workers were clearing the area, a young boy called Errol died after falling under one of the tractors. The neighbourhood went into mourning as parents realised how close their own children came to falling victim to such a tragic accident.

Then a young mentally disabled girl, Marilyn, had wandered away from our school group as we walked home from inter-school sports at a nearby school. Unnoticed by the teachers and other children, Marilyn was abducted when she strayed from the group. Two agonising days later her battered body washed up on Strandfontein, a beach not far from where Mum worked.

For several weeks mothers in the neighbourhood kept a watchful eye as children walked home from school. Mum forbade us to play outside until news broke that the perpetrators had been caught.

Another child, Trevor, in his haste to get to the other side, slipped on the pole and fell into the ravine. When he pulled himself up, a broken glass bottle had pierced his foot. His brother and another boy carried him home, leaving a trail of blood in the sand.

Trevor, who was my age, hobbled around for the next few days, his leg covered in strips of bandage and yellow ointment stains. As the weeks passed he became less mobile and sat around watching us play. Then he no longer came outside.

One morning I followed the other children to where neighbours had gathered outside Trevor's house. 'He died this morning,' one of the neighbours said. 'He had lock-jaw and he died in his sleep.'

As the crowd grew I felt a strange sensation in my jaw. My eyes scanned the crowd searching for Georgie; the tightness spread along my jaw down my neck. Gripped with fear I ran home.

'Frances, Frances, I think I have lock-jaw.'

Frances stood at the kitchen sink, she had just dried cups and plates and was busy wiping the sink. Staring through the window, she pulled the plug to let the water out of the basin.

'I am going to the butcher to fetch the meat,' she said. 'Stay here with Andy and Maureen until I get back.'

I sat in our bedroom for a while, clutching my jaw, my heart beating wildly. Panicked, I grabbed Maureen and Andy by the hand and rushed out of the house in search of Mum. I knew the way to Kleyweg where she worked in the bakery. I had to get to Mum before my jaw locked. Crossing the busy roads, with Maureen and Andy trailing behind me, we walked for more than an hour to Kleyweg, near Muizenberg.

The surprise and horror on Mum's face soon disappeared when I tearfully explained that Trevor had died of lock jaw. The fear of suffering the same fate was etched on my face. After feeding us sandwiches and milk, Mrs Kleyweg gave Mum the afternoon off to take us home.

The council workers continued clearing the land, leaving the whole area flattened. A few weeks later, work commenced on extending our street over the ravine and the pipe disappeared. Shortly after, roads in the new area were completed and land divided into plots for more homes to be built.

After the tractors had left, our extended playground allowed us to roam the flattened area as far as the railway line. Along our side of the railway line, small cottages for coloured railway workers lined the street.

'Only white families can live there on the other side,' Dad told us. 'The main street runs from town to Simonstown. It is about 25 miles long from one end of town to the other.'

5

COMMUNITY AND FAITH

That same year, the council opened a community centre in our area. Mum enrolled me in ballet classes and every Tuesday afternoon I would walk to the community centre with a few girls from the neighbourhood. Mum proudly announced to other neighbourhood mothers that I was doing ballet and encouraged Mrs Oliver to send Cheryl.

'Berenice is doing gymnastics but I need Cheryl at home in the afternoon,' Mrs Oliver said.

Berenice, Cheryl's younger sister, a petite girl with great flexibility, excelled in gymnastics. She was soon able to contort her body to perform daring moves like chin stands, backflips and walking on her hands with her legs extended in the air.

Whenever we visited Mum's older sister, Aunty Susie, she would take us next door to Mrs Parker who played piano. 'Come on, show them the ballet steps,' Mum persuaded.

Even though my movements were awkward and out of rhythm, Mum clapped, beaming with pride while Mrs Parker played. I was more interested in watching her fingers lightly touch the keys than doing ballet.

Around my ninth birthday, Mum befriended my teacher, Miss Essau, who had moved from Worcester, a country town about 120 kilometres from Cape Town.

Miss Essau, desperately unhappy, confided in Mum about her search for a place to stay. Mum sensed the urgency and offered her a temporary bed in our house. Georgie slept in the lounge and Frances, Maureen and I shared the room with Miss Essau.

This was a turning point in our lives. Miss Essau, a devout Catholic, went to Holy Mass every Sunday morning.

'The three older children should have received Holy Communion by now,' she told Mum.

'Mr Crosher won't allow us to return to the Church,' Mum explained. 'I have tried many times over the years but he refuses to go back to the Church.'

'I am a teacher, let me try,' coaxed Ms Essau. 'Coming from someone else he may agree.'

She broached the subject with Dad, who reluctantly agreed. From then on, we accompanied her every Sunday morning. Soon we started attending Catechism classes. Dad had mellowed and presented no objection when Mum announced that we would be receiving our first Holy Communion and Frances would be confirmed. He still refused to attend Holy Mass but allowed us to continue preparation. Frances and I were able to get dresses from the daughters of one of Mum's friends. I wore Shirley's beautiful knee-length white lace dress with a veil and flowers in my hair, and Frances wore Pam's two-piece suit. Georgie, dressed in a white shirt, red tie and his school shorts, looked solemn during the procession to receive our First Communion.

That was the beginning of us practising our faith openly.

Our parish priest welcomed us back into the church and regularly visited our home.

'We could apply for an annulment of your first marriage, Mr Crosher,' the priest offered. 'You were married for only a short time to your first wife and that can be grounds for an annulment; but it is not an easy process.'

But Dad remained aloof and uninterested in the Church. Mum, who could not hide her joy, eagerly attended Holy Mass, even though she was excluded from the Sacraments.

Miss Essau invited us home to Worcester during the school holiday. We boarded the country train for the long ride. Suffering travel sickness shortly after the train left Cape Town Station, I slept most of the way. I remained in bed during the first few days with Miss Essau's mother fussing about me and treating me with all sorts of home remedies.

Their large house, on Le Sueur Street, had a big backyard with many fruit trees. We were allowed to explore the area and met many of their friends.

Miss Essau taught me for the rest of that year. She ensured that we studied at home and took us to the library whenever she could. My results that year was top of the class and she instilled in me a life-long love of spelling and reading. Miss Essau stayed with us until the end of that year when she found a more suitable place to stay.

Later in 1966, some of the mothers in the community, who worked as housemaids for white families on the other side of the railway line, spread the news of a new supermarket in a white area called Bergvliet.

'It's a big supermarket with wide aisles where you can choose your own groceries,' they explained to the mothers.

'Tin food is cheaper and they have a variety of other food stuff,' they explained to Mum.

Only white families could live in the area, but non-white families could do their shopping there.

One Saturday, Frances and I ventured to the supermarket. Walking along the tree-lined streets we looked at the beautiful houses. Everything looked quiet and calm compared to our streets.

On our way back, we stopped to watch the activities at Zwaanswyk, a white high school in a Dutch-style building with immaculately kept rolling lawns. Peering through the wire fence we watched as the cadets marched up and down in neat rows following the commands of the instructor. Inside the school grounds, people sat on chairs or on the lawn, clapping as the cadets marched past.

The school, painted white, gleamed in the sunlight. The vast grounds looked so much neater than schools in our areas.

'Why can't we go to this school?' I asked Frances. 'We can all walk together when I start high school. We don't have to go to your high school.'

'You have to be white to go to this school,' Frances explained. 'Like these people. Look at their skin colour and hair, it's different to ours. Don't tell Dad I said that,' she said sternly. 'Promise me that you won't tell Dad that I said they are different to us.'

Nodding my head to assure her, we stood for a while longer before walking back home. Little did we know that these cadets were in training for future deployment to the South African borders to fight the banned African National Congress of Chief Luthuli and Nelson Mandela."

One Saturday, while Dad was at work, Frances listened to a music request programme on the radio dedicated to the defence force personnel who were out defending the borders. Only white young men were conscripted to the army. The messages from family and girlfriends were always the same: *Min dae, baie hare.* I had no idea what this meant until much later when I found out that it referred to counting the days and growing their hair.

Dad would have been horrified if he knew that we were listening. 'They are not protecting us on the borders,' Dad would say adamantly. 'They are fighting to protect this land for themselves.'

On Tuesdays, when he was relaxed, Dad would discuss the government's policies in between drinking and reading the newspapers. Because of his good command of the English language, he mixed with tourists and business people at the hotel and learned a lot more about world affairs.

At the time, while I did not understand South Africa's involvement in South West Africa, although, Dad talked to us as if we understood. The South West African People's Organisation (SWAPO) was formed as a resistance movement which for many years fought for Namibian independence. In the early 1960s SWAPO was the main threat to South Africa's borders.

Critical of the government's enforcement of the same apartheid policies in South West Africa, Dad supported those who were fighting for freedom. It was as if he was defending St Helena situated on the same west coast.

With a cigarette hanging from his mouth he would say, 'This government don't know what they are doing. Moving blacks out into separate homelands, the government wants them to destroy themselves. Putting the coloured people around the coast, will position us in the firing line should there ever be an attack from the sea. This way they can keep all of us under control.'

'Oh Ben, stop trying to fill their heads with your nonsense,' Mum would retort. 'Why don't you help them with their school work instead of telling them things that we can do nothing about.'

But, at every opportunity Dad condemned the government's separate development plans.

Under the Bantu Homelands Citizens Act, ten separate Bantu homelands had been created across the county to move blacks out of the cities. This allowed the government to reinforce their inhumane segregation policies to separate blacks and deny them their rights as South African nationals, including their right to work and live in South Africa. That would also prevent them from forming a single unifying majority group.

Black people who had the necessary temporary work permits could live in the townships on the outskirts of the city, but their wives and families had to remain in the homelands. At the end of the year, bus-loads of black workers travelled back to the Transkei to spend their annual holidays with their families. The closest Bantu homeland for blacks working in Cape Town was the Transkei in the south-eastern Cape.

Dad talked briefly about Nelson Mandela and other members of the banned African National Congress who had been convicted of treason. I was only eight years old at the time, and many of the political discussions Dad had was beyond my comprehension. Following Nelson Mandela's imprisonment, the government banned every trace of his existence. In the Cape, his name was always whispered among those who were actively involved in politics.

When South Africa became a republic in 1961, all schools were compelled to sing the Afrikaans national anthem, *Die Stem van Suid-Afrika* or *The Call of South Africa,* at assembly. Republic Day on 31 May was a day of celebration for white people—and a day off for us who boycotted it.

The hoisting of the flag lasted for several years, until one day, in a move of defiance, coloured school principals scrapped the practice of singing the anthem and hoisting the flag on school property.

The systematic removal of non-whites under the Group Areas Act continued through the 1960s. The pain and separation engulfed our communities with the inhumane upheaval of many families.

Perhaps the most controversial was when District Six, an inner-city area, was declared a white area in 1966. More than 60,000 'non-white' families were forcibly removed.

In keeping with the apartheid philosophy, one of the government's primary reasons for these removals was that interracial interaction bred conflict. For this reason, the government felt it necessary to separate the races. There were other official reasons such as declaring the area a slum and a place full of immoral activities.

Dad read every bit of news surrounding this controversial move, which also attracted international attention. He was very vocal about the government's main reason being the prime location of District Six: its proximity to the city centre, Table Mountain, and the harbour.

The forced removals started in 1968 with the estimated 60,000 people relocated to the sandy, bleak Cape Flats townships some 25 kilometres away. The old houses were bulldozed and the only buildings left were the mosque and churches.

The government's plans for redevelopment of the area were thwarted by international and local pressure and the vacant land remained undeveloped for a few decades —much of it still lies vacant even now.

It was only when I watched the poignant stage musical *District Six*, produced by Taliep Petersen and David Kramer, about the forced removals of these families that I understood and felt their pain. A whole community had been uprooted by these skewed apartheid policies. How could these people live with themselves when they caused so much pain and heartache?

When the government claimed District Six, the community lost its sense of belonging. The Kaapse Klopse, a cultural festival also referred to as the Coon Carnival, had lost its home.

Tweede Nuwe Jaar ('Second New Year', on the 2nd of January) is a day that is unique to the Cape. The Kaapse Klopse carnival stems from our Cape Malay slave history.

On that day, slaves were given a day off work and this alternate New Year celebration became an iconic street festival of song and dance with colourful costumes, ghoema drums, guitars and penny-whistles. Over the years, the local working-class community, which survived slavery and endured apartheid, commemorated the struggle and their determination through this street parade.

Scatterlings of Cape Malays who lived in our area formed their troupes and filled our streets with their costumes, song and dance in preparation for the big festival.

As children, we gathered in the streets to watch them go through their paces until they stopped at the Jeptha home to continue their rehearsals.

With the entire inner-city centre declared white, the parade through the city was banned. The performances were then spread across the Cape Peninsula to various areas, instead of the usual route across the city centre from District Six to Green Point Stadium.

With non-whites now spread across a vast area of the Cape Flats, transport costs to attend this celebration became a challenge. When the government imposed the Illegal Gathering Act in the early 1970s, it placed additional challenges on the festival organisers and led to the event being held in non-white areas and only for non-white spectators.

By 1977, all Kaapse Klopse marches were considered unsavoury and banned by the government. The event was then moved between various stadiums to keep it alive until 1989, when after pressure from many sectors of the community the event returned to its original route, from (now demolished) District Six to Green Point.

Despite our limitations, we created our own fun and games. At the age of 11 I staged my first backyard concert, charging children in the area half a cent to see the performance. Berenice was my star performer; with her flexible body she was fearless and knew no limits. Those who could not afford the half cent came in for free and sat in the back.

Dancing and contorting our bodies, we entertained the audience with our skill, performing daring flips and pyramids. A pure wonder that we didn't break any bones or dislocate any body parts.

Mrs Daniels, a lady in our neighbourhood, heard about my successful concerts and invited me to do a joint concert with her daughter at their house. 'We'll charge a fee and give your team some of the money,' she said.

I set about training in secrecy, confident that we had Berenice on our team as the star attraction. On the day of the concert, I arrived at the house with my team of eight-to--eleven-year-old competitors. Many neighbours crammed into the small lounge, clapping and cheering loudly as we carried out some risky moves. The concert was a huge success.

'We will hold another concert soon and all that money will be yours,' Mrs Daniels explained. Disappointed, we left empty-handed, but I promised my team that we would continue with our own concerts and make it bigger and better.

One thing we learned never to say around Mum was that we were bored. The first place Mum would send us was the library. Steenberg Library was the only one servicing our area. I devoured books by my favourite author, Enid Blyton, and the librarian often kept copies of new books for me to collect. My favourite Enid Blyton book was *The Enchanted Wood*. All my English essays centred on adventures in the bush, areas I was familiar with.

Frances would make piles of apricot jam sandwiches and we'd spend hours laying on our beds reading.

Mum was at her happiest when we were reading and talking about books.

6

THE RED WIRELESS

On Tuesdays, Dad listened to Springbok Radio and sometimes tuned into Lourenço Marques (LM) Radio. It was the one day of the week when he would cook his favourite dishes, such as black-eyed beans curry, tomato bredie, cabbage stew or curried meatballs.

With a Van Rijn unfiltered cigarette always close at hand, he would puff away while he filled his glass with wine throughout the day. By lunch time he would be ready to take a nap.

Benjamin George Crosher was born on 15 July 1914 on the island of St Helena, one of the most remote places in the world, situated off the west coast of Africa. One of four children, his heritage is linked to that of East Indian slave descent.

Tall and lean, with dark unruly curls, dark brown skin and distinct Asian features, his first language was English.

He had a haughtiness about him, was always immaculately dressed in starched white shirts and pressed pants
with his favourite accessory, a pair of braces. His hair
was neatly sleeked back with Brylcreem, highlighting his
slanty eyes, his mouth filled with cigarette stained teeth.

The crackling sound of the red wireless was always
a sign that Dad was awake, laying in bed, smoking. The
aerial, a thin wire strung across the dressing table mirror, was carefully positioned near the window for clearer
reception.

The wireless fitted perfectly on the imbuia dress-
ing-table on top of Mum's lace doyley. A yellowing mesh
covered the front panel, the brown wooden knobs were
worn and carefully glued onto the metal prongs, allowing
Dad to tune the radio and adjust the volume.

The Wynberg Hotel van delivered his order every
Tuesday. A gallon of Lieberstein, a sweet white wine, and
a bottle of Viceroy Brandy, which usually lasted until the
next delivery. The gallon had a little hook on top making
it easier for Dad to push his finger through when carrying
it. Dad worked long hours and never drank during the
week, but Tuesdays was his drinking day.

In the evening, he listened to *Call Back the Past,* and
later all five of us joined him on the double-bed listening
to the courtroom drama *Consider Your Verdict.* Waiting
for the voice to announce, 'it's time to take your place
on the jury', Dad would ask all of us for our verdict while
we waited with bated breath to hear the words 'guilty' or
'not guilty'. Dad always knew what the verdict was but
gave us a chance to give our verdict first.

Tuesdays was also the day when his hair was free of
Brylcreem. He would allow us to take turns combing and

styling his long locks into ponytails with ribbons and hair pins in it.

We knew very little about Dad's family, or his birth family name, except that his parents were descendants of East Indian slaves. Dad's stories of his family succumbing to the tuberculosis epidemic were often relayed when he had been drinking. He was the sole survivor and was adopted at the age of 12 by an Englishman, Mr Crosher, who moved to Cape Town.

Mr Crosher settled on farmlands in an area called Varkensvlei, in the southern suburbs. This small area of land surrounded by coloured areas was allocated to white farmers because of the rich soil. Dad attended the newly-built Livingstone High School in 1927. He spent his spare time helping on the farm, feeding the chickens and cleaning pigsties.

He had wanted to train as a teacher, but Mr Crosher died before Dad finished high school, leaving him to fend for himself. He moved in with the Bailey family, who were also from St Helena, and lived with them until his first marriage. The childless marriage lasted for 18 months before they divorced and she moved to England.

With an unfulfilled dream of teaching and a sense of abandonment, he drifted from one hotel to another, working as a wine steward.

In May 1951 he met Mum on the train to work. At the time, Dad worked at St James Hotel, a popular tourist hotel along the False Bay Coast. Mum worked as a live-in housemaid at the Marina Hotel in Muizenberg. A brief courtship followed and they married in March 1952. Dad continued to work at the St James Hotel for a few years until he found a job as a barman at the Wynberg Hotel.

An avid reader, Dad had many historical books and scanned the newspapers from front page to back page. His interests centred around colonial history, war stories and sports. Crossword puzzles, betting on the horses and the wireless were Dad's escape into the world outside of work.

A loner with no ties to family or friends, he preferred his own company and that of his children. Dad did not fraternise with neighbours and we never went out as a family.

While Dad spoke *only* English, Mum was from an Afrikaans-speaking family. He refused to communicate in Afrikaans, the language of the government, and detested going into public offices, like the Post Office, where the workers were all Afrikaners. The humiliation of having to walk through a marked entrance and then to communicate in Afrikaans infuriated him.

'The Saints use the Queen's English and they don't understand a word of it,' he would often remark, indicating Afrikaners.

Politically and historically, Afrikaans has often been seen as a controversial language. We grew up communicating with Dad in English and with Mum in Afrikaans. In our schooling we were taught in Afrikaans, and depending on whom we played with, we'd switched to either language. My older cousins spoke Afrikaans and some of the younger ones English. This is the reason why many of us grew up mixing the two languages, even in mid-sentence. This was commonly referred to as *Kombuis Afrikaans*, or 'kitchen Afrikaans'. There are several ways of speaking Afrikaans, depending on where you grew up.

'Your mother is a Cape Coloured,' Dad would often chuckle to tease Mum. 'You know why? Her father is

Portuguese and her mother is black. That makes them coloured. That is why when they speak Afrikaans, it is with a uvular trill; they call it *brey*.'

'Oh, don't listen to your father,' was Mum's only response. 'He doesn't even know where his parents are from. Ask him to explain.'

'I am a foreigner,' he would proudly say. 'My grand-parents came from East India and arrived on big ships as slaves. After my parents died, I should have gone to England, Australia or Canada. That would have been bet-ter than living here in this country.'

It was during those times that Dad revealed little bits about his background. It was evident that his life was riddled with difficult and painful memories which he was reluctant to disclose. His struggle with displacement and a consciousness of class and colour was clear to see.

A sports lover, Dad taught us about cricket and rugby. Whenever possible he would listen to radio broad-caster Charles Fortune, who was known as the voice of South African cricket.

'I could never play for the school cricket team,' Dad said sadly. 'Every afternoon I had to rush home to help on the farm.'

Rugby was his other passion. His favourite team was the British Lions and he backed any team who played against the white national team, the Springboks. Non-whites were not allowed to represent South Africa at international level. Dad ranted and expressed his disgust at the racial segregation and the missed opportunities for talented coloured sports people.

Mum and Dad had different ways of coping with the political situation.

My mother was born Sarah Stebes (later changed to Stevens) in 1930. Her pragmatic nature in life was a result of being raised in a large family. Mum's life from childhood into adulthood was one of survival. This instilled in her a determination to succeed. As was common in those days, Mum left school at a young age. Eager to learn, she possessed a sensitivity that drew others towards her.

Her survival instincts were put to the test on the day she gave birth to Frances, her first-born, Dad was involved in a car accident while out celebrating with work colleagues. He spent several months in hospital, leaving Mum to survive with a newborn and with limited resources. Young and without support, she fended for herself and the baby. When Dad was discharged, they moved into my grandparents' house in Retreat.

Mum approached life differently to Dad. She tried her hand at anything, be it fixing things in the house or growing vegetables in the backyard. While she did not accept the classification that the government labelled her with, that of a Cape Coloured, it was not her focus. She dealt with it in the only way she could: to ensure that our lives would be different to hers. She believed that education would be the key to a better future for us.

Dad continually cursed the evils of apartheid because of the limitations it placed on him. He resented that he had to leave St Helena and yearned for a life that he could never get back. He was trapped by his belief that his life could have been better had he not left St Helena.

At every opportunity, he educated us about the evils of apartheid and how he wished the worst on the government. He dreamed of a better life, but that is all it was: dreams.

Mum was desperate for normalcy in the home. She was focussed on raising her family, and making ends meet to survive.

'We can't change the laws,' she would remind Dad. 'We must focus on our own lives; our everyday life and how to get through it week by week.'

Dad, well-read and socially mixing in other circles at work, was forthright and outspoken about his views. He harboured hatred and an intense dislike more for Afrikaners than for English-speaking white people. His boss, Mr Freedberg, a Jew, afforded Dad many privileges, such as driving his car and luxuries like food and drink. Dad would walk around with his hand in his trouser pocket jingling the many coins he received as tips. That was his riches.

One day that stands out is Tuesday, the 6th of September 1966. I arrived home from school to find Dad glued to the wireless. He was moving the aerial from side to side, muttering to himself that the wind was causing the poor reception. Motioning me to be quiet, I heard beeping sounds and then a voice announcing: 'Prime Minister Hendrik Verwoerd has been attacked!'

Dr Verwoerd was known as the 'Architect of Apartheid' for his role in shaping and implementing the apartheid policy. He had led the white Nationalist government which approved of his plan to preserve the white population as the 'master race'. His grand plan was to divide people by the colour of their skin through introducing oppressive laws which diminished the rights of non-white South Africans. His reign was brutal—those in opposition to his plans—killed or exiled.

The Sharpeville massacre, in the Transvaal Province

in northern South Africa, on 21 March 1960, was one of the most brutal events during his reign as Prime Minister.

In Sharpeville a day of demonstrations against the pass laws—an internal identification system to further segregate black people—led to protesters storming the local police station. Dr Verwoerd gave the order for the police to open fire. They killed 69 black African demonstrators. At least 180 were injured, although there are claims that the number was as high as 300.

Dr Verwoerd led the establishment of the Republic of South Africa in 1961 and ruled the country with an iron fist by banning movements such as the African National Congress and other opposing political groups. He was at the helm when ANC leaders were prosecuted in the Rivonia trial that had Nelson Mandela and others jailed.

That September day in 1966, Dad sat in silence listening intently, turning up the sound each time the beeps sounded. The radio announcer repeated the same message, 'Prime Minister Verwoerd has been attacked in Parliament.'

When Frances and Georgie arrived, we sat quietly while he listened to each broadcast. Unlike other afternoons, Dad did not hover around the table while we ate. Instead, he stayed in the bedroom, close to the wireless while staring blankly at the wall or out of the window at the mountains in the distance.

As the afternoon progressed, Dad heard on the news that Prime Minister Verwoerd had died by assassination. In between broadcasts he stood at the front door, leaning on his one arm against the frame, as if he was waiting for someone to come through the gate.

Then finally he turned to us and said, 'That evil man

Verwoerd is dead, stabbed in the neck like a pig. This is the second attempt on his life and now they finally killed him, right in Parliament where he passed all these laws against us.'

None of us understood the status of the deceased and what a significant moment in South African history it was. Dad continued listening to the radio broadcasts until Mum arrived home earlier than usual.

Mum said that Mrs Kleyweg cried and closed the bakery when she heard the news. She sat listening as Dad filled her in on the day's events. They talked earnestly about what this could mean, and the possibility that the next Prime Minister might make changes.

'There are people in his own party who do not agree with him,' said Dad. 'This could be the time for them to make changes.'

That day, we bathed early and sat quietly on the bed while they listened to the evening news. Our neighbour Mr Oliver visited, and for the first time since we had moved in two years ago Dad shared a few glasses of wine with him.

'Yes, Mr Crosher, the government moved us out of Bo-Kaap against our will. We all lived happily together there: whites, Malays, black and coloured people. The sad thing is that it turned neighbours against each other. Those whites who were privileged to remain in the area were our friends, we lived side-by-side for many years. But when the government told us we had to move, they did not support us; instead they watched how we packed up and moved out. We had no say. My wife's sister and her family had to move to the flats in a place called Manenberg.'

Mr Oliver continued, 'I worked close by in Wood-stock and all my working life I could walk to work. Now I must get up early to travel to work. I don't see my mother as often and all our friends moved to different places. My mother is still waiting for a house.'

As more news were released over the following days, Verwoerd's assassin was identified as Dimitri Tsafendas, the son of a Greek seaman and a Mozambican mother of mixed race. He was classified as white and worked as a parliamentary messenger, giving him direct access to the Prime Minister in the chambers. He was later found not guilty by reason of insanity.

Dad was on two weeks' holidays and read every bit of news about the assassination. He balked at the thousands of white people who attended the funeral and showed us newspaper pictures of how they lined the streets.

That Sunday evening I knew it was time for Dad to return to work when he polished his shoes, and I heard the hissing sound the hot iron made when it touched the wet cloth as he pressed his black pants. The next morning he left for work and it was as if nothing had happened; he never spoke about the news again. And Mr Oliver never visited again.

But what didn't change was us listening to the little red wireless, the only source of family entertainment. Before bedtime we would pile onto Mum and Dad's double bed to listen to our favourite programs.

On Monday nights, we listened to the popular game show *Pick a Box* and the familiar line "the money or the box" had us screaming out our advice to the contestant. Other popular shows were *No Place to Hide*, featuring private investigator Mark Saxon, and Friday evenings, the familiar catch phrase "… they prowl the empty streets at night" signalled the start of a *Squad Cars*.

Dad, an asthma sufferer, had started spending a lot of time off work, especially during the rainy winter months. He also had severe eczema and kept his skin covered with a thick white ointment to stop the itching and sores. Dr Moss often visited our house to treat him, leaving a prescription for the little orange-and-blue Amesac capsules to help open Dad's bronchial pipes.

'You must stop smoking, Mr Crosher,' Dr Moss urged. 'Your children are still very young and you must stay healthy to work for them.'

But he didn't stop smoking and as the months passed, Dad's attacks became more and more frequent, rendering him unable to work for weeks. His boss, Mr Freedberg, sent Dad money and groceries every Tuesday for several weeks and the driver would deliver his wine.

I worried about Dad's coughing and would carry glasses of water to his bed whenever he had a coughing fit. With his appearance ungroomed, he looked drawn and tired; most days he would remain in bed and hardly ate.

Mum's day started at 6 am. Most days she would get home at 6 pm, or later if she worked at catering functions. Kleyweg bakery catered for wealthy white people. Some of these parties were for clients like the world-famous heart surgeon Dr Christiaan Barnard, and other dignitaries like United Party leader Sir De Villiers Graaf. Whenever Mum worked at these parties, she would receive tips to supplement her income and bring home left-over food parcels. These food parcels would be shared with our neighbour.

One afternoon in April 1968, it was unusual for us to find Dad home. On the kitchen table stood a big box of groceries and a box filled with Dad's usual wine and brandy. He didn't say much to us and sat listening to the radio until Mum arrived later that evening.

From behind the closed door in their bedroom we heard his muffled cries, 'I am so sorry, Sarah, I am so sorry. Mr Freedberg gave me some extra money and the box of groceries. I will be able to do some casual work at the hotel when I feel better. Mr Freedberg will help me to apply for a disability grant at the Coloured Affairs office.'

In the darkness, we lay quietly in our room. Georgie, on his back staring at the ceiling. In the bunk below, with the lace curtain around her bunk drawn, Frances lay. Maureen and Andy were already asleep. Tears rolled down my cheeks as I listened to Dad's wheezing chest and muffled cries.

Struggling to keep his composure he said again, 'After the winter months, and with some rest I will be able to go back to work.'

'I know, Ben,' Mum said reassuringly.

Earlier that evening I peered through the crack in their bedroom door; Mum put Dad's money in their wardrobe between some clothes. Cursing his sick body, his voice crackling, Dad worried about what would happen to us without his income.

'Everything will be alright, Ben,' said Mum. 'I can get extra shifts and do evening catering. You take care of the house and the children. We won't need Mrs Hannie anymore.'

Over the next few months Dad took care of us at home. The hotel delivery van continued to drop off his box of wine every Tuesday. Dr Moss regularly came to our house as Dad struggled during that winter.

Despite what was happening at home, we all excelled at school. Mum proudly displayed the white folded report cards and book prizes we received. Some of Mum's sisters, who at times would send groceries to help us, withdrew their help when Mum refused to take Frances and Georgie out of school to help her financially.

'My children will not do menial work in factories while I am still alive,' Mum retorted. 'Look at these two feet and these two hands—I will work them to the bone to educate my children and to keep a roof over our heads.'

She continued to work long hours and we hardly saw her during the week. It was comforting to have Dad at home to help us with homework and to have a warm meal waiting for us. But Dad was not coping. He would retire to bed early and bouts of coughing would rack his body as his bronchial tubes tightened.

Christmas was a time when the neighbourhood would be abuzz with people busily cleaning their homes. Lace curtains filling washing lines flapped in the air. The strong smell of paint hung in the air whenever we passed neighbourhood homes. Christmas choirs and bands walking down the streets created the festive atmosphere.

Mum tried her best to make it a special time. Even though she worked long hours, and with her limited budget, she baked a sweet cookie called Kolwyntjies, and made ginger beer brewed with pineapples. This brew was prepared a few weeks before and stored in bottles in the cupboard. One Christmas the concoction was so potent that several bottles exploded, leaving us with only a few to share.

We could never afford cases of Bashews, the colourful bottles of fizzy cold drinks that some families in our neighbourhood bought at Christmas or special occasions.

That Christmas, his first one at home, Dad did not get out of bed to have lunch with us. The smell of roast chicken filtered into our room. In the kitchen Mum was preparing Christmas lunch. Sweet yellow rice and raisins, roast potatoes, and gravy stood on the stove. She had prepared beetroot and onion salad the night before. The red jelly Mum had made stood overnight on the cement slab in the bathroom to set—the coolest place in the house.

The five of us could fit around the dining table and the race was always on to get the squeaky chair. This was a highlight until Mum made the squeaker stop. Mum and Dad waited until we had eaten before dining on the leftovers.

For us, the day was no different to any other day. We didn't have Christmas decorations nor new clothes, as most of the neighbourhood children had.

Hearing the high-pitched voices of the girls next door, Frances whispered, 'Quick, close the door.'

But before I could climb down from the top bunk, Mum called us to the lounge room.

'Frances, Beryl, the Oliver girls are here to wish us for Christmas.'

'Merry Christmas, Mrs Crosher,' we heard them say in unison.

Slowly, I climbed down and tried to pull Frances out of her bed, but she pulled the blanket over her head.

Opening the lace curtain I dragged her out of bed. Slipping on my old shoes, I whispered, 'Brush your hair and tie it before we go inside.'

In the lounge, the Oliver girls, dressed in beautiful clothes, stood in a row according to their height. They wore hats and matching bags, gloves and new patent leather shoes. Cheryl stood third from the left, looking pretty with her hat perched and her long hair hanging down her back.

'Merry Christmas,' they said in unison.

Frances, squeezed in behind my back, using me as a shield to hide her old dress. She placed her head on my shoulder so that only her face was visible.

Softly, we responded, 'Merry Christmas.'

Cheryl smiled at me, but I could not take my eyes off their hats, bags and white gloves. They stood for a few moments longer while we looked at them in an uncomfortable silence. I shuffled behind the chair trying to hide my old shoes. As soon as they moved towards the door, we slipped back into our room. Without saying a word Frances crept into her bed and closed the lace curtain.

I could hear her sighing. Georgie tried to make us laugh by putting a bowl on his head and Mum's bag over his arm. 'Merry Christmas,' he mocked in a high-pitched voice.

'As soon as I get a job, then I will buy us new clothes every year,' Frances said. 'I have two more years at school before I can start looking.'

'Cheryl had such a beautiful dress,' I said. 'They all looked so pretty in their Christmas clothes.'

I reached for the door to our small blue wardrobe. Inside hung my brand-new high school uniform: a navy pleated skirt, white blouse and a navy blazer. Running my finger over the yellow and blue cotton on the badge on the upper left-hand pocket, I traced the words, '*Per Laborem Ad Astra*', a phrase meaning 'Through Hard Work to the Stars'.

At the bottom of the cupboard stood the boxes with our new school shoes ready for the start of school in early January 1969. In my head, I could hear Mum's words: *If you have a good education then you will get a good job and will then be able to buy the things that you want.*

As we did every Sunday after lunch, the three of us walked down to our cousins living at Princess Vlei, a lake in 11th Avenue. It was an hour's walk over the sand hills past my grandparents' old house. Almost ten years had passed since we had moved out, but the chimney was still standing. To keep us entertained along the way, Georgie made up games and stories.

Our cousins Eddie, Norman, Gene and Eleanor had moved back to join other cousins living in a property at the lake in Retreat. The owners of the property, a Dutch couple, had to move out after the Group Areas Act was imposed. Unlike non-white people, who had to sell and move out of areas zoned as white, white people could continue as property owners in non-white areas.

I loved the wide-open spaces, the hills and the windmill. Playing in the lake was forbidden. There had been many drownings and we were warned about quicksand that sucked people in. I joined my cousins running around on the hills on the small holding. We would take turns to ride on the unbridled horse or feed the chickens, ducks and pigs.

In January 1969, two days before high school opened, Dad took me for enrolment day at Steenberg High. Mr Lochner, the coloured principal with a reputation for being a tough disciplinarian, addressed Dad in Afrikaans.

Dad immediately turned on his haughty English tone and said, 'This is my daughter, Beryl Crosher. She was enrolled through her primary school into Standard 6 [Grade 8]. I would like her to change to the English class.'

Mr Lochner looked at Dad and continued in Afrikaans, 'No, your daughter must remain in the Afrikaans class.' Looking at Dad intently, he said, 'You speak Afrikaans at home, she has done all her schooling so far in Afrikaans, therefore she must remain in the Afrikaans class.'

Shifting around, I watched Dad's reaction. With his eyes firmly fixed on Mr Lochner and his jaw clenched he said, 'You shall address me in English at all times.'

Pointing at me, he snarled 'They are the Japies, not me.'

Japies, shortened from 'plaas japies', was a term given to Afrikaner farmers or people from the country towns.

Mr Lochner looked down at his desk and reluctantly switched to English to reinforce his decision. While Dad and Mr Lochner engaged in a stand-off, I looked down at my shoes, praying for the moment to pass. For Dad, Afrikaans was a reminder of the oppressive government. It was an official language and the first language of the ruling party.

Signs on public places were displayed in Afrikaans and English. The clear majority of front-line public service jobs were held by white people, mainly Afrikaners. It was seen as an act of defiance to address a white official in English.

My first day of high school finally dawned. Mum had taken the day off and proudly stood at the gate smiling as the five of us walked down the road. Careful not to get dust on my shoes, I jumped on the patches of grass down the side driveway.

'Enjoy your first day at high school,' she said to me. 'Look after Beryl,' she said to Frances and Georgie.

Touching my new, crisp pleated skirt and blazer, I felt grown up in the company of my older siblings. My black shoes gleamed in the sunlight and my new sparkling white socks folded at the ankles. Frances had straightened the blue ribbons in my plaited hair before we walked out of the house. Andy and Maureen, dressed in their new green uniforms, walked across the road to Harmony Primary.

I stopped to see if Cheryl was ready to go to high school, but only her younger sisters walked across the road to the primary school.

'Where is Cheryl?' I asked.

'She went to work this morning.'

Instead of joining me in high school, Cheryl and some of my other thirteen-year-old friends started work on production lines at clothing factories like Rex True-form, Monatic and TEJ. While my school satchel was filled with exercise books and textbooks, Cheryl and the other young girls were dressed in casual clothes and carried work bags.

For the first few weeks, I would run to the gate in the early evening to watch Cheryl and the other girls turn the corner at the top of our street. Smiling and waving, Cheryl walked past in the company of her older sister and aunt. One friend wore a pair of boots, white patent leather knee-high, which I secretly envied.

'These children are too young to work. Why don't

you let them study so that they can get better jobs when they are older,' Mum urged their parents.

But to no avail. Although the parents promised that they would send them to night school, they never did.

As the weeks progressed, Cheryl and I grew apart. I hardly saw her and she spent more time in the company of her older sisters. Dressed in adult clothing, she now talked about having a weekly train ticket and working all day in the factory. She was no longer home to meet in the afternoons or to play during the school holidays.

With Frances now in her second-last year of high school, Mum could get her a part-time job at some catering functions. Frances eagerly saved her money to buy us special treats. At school, she was doing needlework and made her first dress and this encouraged her to start sewing clothes for us. Georgie also found a part-time job at a barber shop, and with this extra money Mum could buy a few luxuries.

A young science teacher had started at our school. Tall and lanky, he was only a few years older than Frances. Mr Londt was passionate about teaching and opened up the world of science to us. Through his self-funded experiments he turned the under-equipped science rooms into a vibrant place of learning. Mr Londt befriended Frances and other senior students and would visit our home from time to time. He had this knack, through his passion, to engage everyone in science. We were filled with admiration for his experiments and his enthusiasm to impart his knowledge.

Many teachers, despite the inequalities and under-funding, remained dedicated to their vocation. In high school I learnt more about the differences between us and white students. Teachers openly discussed the impact apartheid had on our education, and many expressed their frustration at the inequality of their recognition as educators.

Through the government's segregation policies, the education funding ratio was unfairly distributed. The three-tiered funding level gave white schools an unfair financial advantage, allowing them to have top class facilities. Non-white schools received substantially less funding, leaving students at a disadvantage. Our high school had science classes without equipment, and teachers often spent their own money on supplies for experiments.

At home Dad supervised our homework. On the days that he didn't drink, he would spend hours talking to us about how *under* apartheid, the government deprived us of the same benefits that white students had.

Whenever Mum heard Dad talking about these inequalities, she'd brush aside his comments about our inferior education—or gutter education, as it was commonly known.

'No child of mine will be carrying trays and washing up piles of dishes after catering jobs,' she would say. 'Whenever I stand at the sink washing the dishes, I think about you children. When I am tired and barely able to cycle home, I think about why I am doing this—how much better things will be for your future lives.'

This made us work harder, not wanting to disappoint her, especially when we watched her treating her sore feet by soaking them in vinegar water and scraping off the hard skin with a Minora blade. She used a remedy given by Uncle Hamad, a family friend, to wrap her feet in banana peels overnight. 'The banana peels will draw the inflammation out of your feet,' he claimed.

Uncle Hamad, a Muslim, lived on a big property and cultivated his own vegetables and fruit. He regularly delivered a box full of his produce, and he too took every opportunity to encourage us to study harder.

My first few weeks at high school were exciting. The school building was much bigger than primary school and was spread out in a u-shaped design, with two levels. In the centre, was a tarred quadrangle where we had assembly every Monday morning. On the side stood the disused flag pole where they *once* raised the South African flag and sang the anthem. The words of the anthem remained in my head, but it had become something that no coloured person spoke of or ever dared to sing.

With us dressed in white shorts and shirts and white sand-shoes, physical education was carried out on the quadrangle. During the cold winter months we shivered during early morning classes. George had the weekly chore of polishing our black shoes and painting our sand-shoes with a whitening paste which, when dry, made them hard to get our feet into. To stretch our sand-shoes, we'd jumped around at home until they fitted comfortably.

Across the quadrangle spread a large open field where the boys played soccer. It also served as our athletics track for the inter-house carnival. The field, mostly covered in gravel, had scattered thorn bushes and little patches of grass. On windy days, the quadrangle offered cover from the dust blowing around. In winter time, the field would turn into a mud bath.

Despite the lack of proper facilities, inadequate

training and virtually no equipment, many young athletes developed into top runners under our dedicated teachers. One such athlete, a barefooted long-distance runner, Desmond Sakinaris, set the track alight with his prowess and went on to represent our province.

Inter-school's carnivals were held at the old cinder track at Green Point Stadium. Here we competed against coloured schools from across the Western Cape in two divisions. This facility was given to us after a bigger, state-of-the-art stadium was built for white students.

Proudly we sang our favourite cheering songs:
'Here we are, here we are, here we are again.
My mother told me, to wear a white short and
a blue shirt to run for Steenberg.'

The highlight of our school's sporting calendar was an event called the 'Champion of Champions'. This gave a platform for coloured athletes to compete with the best in the western Cape. The top athletes were then selected to represent coloured schools at provincial level. They were issued with smart blazers and blue ties that signalled their sporting ability. Steenberg High, despite its sub-economic status, produced several elite level provincial champions. We were proud of our classmate Felicity Singh, who made the provincial team.

There were only two black high schools in the Western Cape and those students did not compete with either white or coloured students.

Because of the segregation policies, separate sporting clubs and governing bodies were established. Only white sporting bodies were affiliated with international sporting bodies, including the International Olympic Committee. This allowed white athletes opportunities to compete abroad. In 1964, South Africa was banned from the Olympics in Tokyo because of the government's refusal to condemn apartheid. In the late 1960s, exclusion of South Africa in the international sporting arena grew.

Many staunch advocates of the ban against South Africa rejoiced at the news of South Africa's expulsion from the international arena. When England cancelled the 1970 South African cricket tour, Dad, who followed sport closely, was torn between his love of cricket and rugby on the one hand, and South Africa's isolation on the other.

Dad's love of sport often clouded his judgment. He remained opposed to the government's divisive sports policy and rejected any concessions the coloured representative body, South African Non-Racial Sports Organisation were willing to agree to. These included maintaining separate sporting bodies.

I learnt from Dad at a young age about the treatment of Maoris who toured with the All Blacks. In 1970, under pressure by the All Blacks Association, the government relented to allow Maoris to be part of the team by bestowing on them the title of 'honorary whites'. This was to meet the team's demands that their players be allowed to stay in the same hotel. Demonstrators both in New Zealand and South Africa voiced their opposition to these concessions as being insulting.

The title 'honorary whites' was also bestowed on people of other ethnic backgrounds. To assist a trade pact, Japanese and other East Asians were included as 'honorary whites'. This allowed them the same privileges as white South Africans. It was only much later that the Chinese were included as 'honorary whites' and afforded the same privileges.

Our teachers, all coloured, talked about the government's unfair policies regarding education and sports funding. Despite their grumblings, Mr Lochner, a strict educator and principal, applied tough rules in relation to discipline and homework. Like Mum, he reminded us that it was not about growing up in Steenberg but that our education would open doors for us in the future.

A significant event happened on 20 July 1969. That day, with Dad, we sat glued to the radio listening to the broadcast of the first landing on the moon. Having looked at the moon so many times it was hard to believe how someone could reach the moon and walk on it.

As we gathered around the small red crackling radio, astronaut Neil Armstrong said those significant words, 'One small step for man, one giant leap for mankind.' Dad reinforced in us how significant this moment would become in our history.

Despite his ill health, Dad would get dressed in his white shirt, black pants and maroon braces and wear his favourite maroon cardigan on cooler days. In winter time, he wore a grandpa vest under his shirt and long johns to ward off the cold.

On days when Dad felt well enough, the table would be set and there'd always be a cooked meal waiting for us in the afternoon. Fussing around the table, Dad watched while we ate, encouraging us to chew our food 36 times before swallowing.

My first year of high school passed very quickly. Soon Frances was in matric. My cousin Norman, a cabinet maker, arranged for an apprenticeship for Georgie, who had completed Grade 10. It was one of Mum's proudest days when his papers arrived to show his status as an indentured apprentice cabinet maker.

Most evenings Georgie would return home with interesting tales about being an apprentice. We'd listen, fascinated, to descriptions of timbers and tools, the people he worked with, and how to remove wood splinters.

That year, Frances moved her bed out of the shared bedroom into the lounge room so that she could have more privacy. She saved her money to buy fabric to sew clothes for us. Her needlework classes at school had given her the skills to cut and sew skirts and dresses. Flared pants, short skirts and hot pants, and later boleros and mid-length skirts. To save on fabric costs she made identical skirts or hot pants using the same pattern.

At the start of Grade 9, I befriended Geraldine. She lived in a squatter camp near Steenberg Station among rows of wood and iron houses, without electricity, running water or sewage. Geraldine, quietly spoken and always immaculately groomed, was the brightest student in the entire school. She was the only student at the time who was awarded a bursary to study at university.

Both Geraldine and I talked about studying teaching and I was inspired by her diligence and ability to quickly grasp maths concepts. She helped me with maths and spent time showing me complex algebra and geometry calculations. Her lack of adequate facilities at home did little to deter her determination to achieve her dream. Completing her homework by candlelight, and carrying buckets of water from a communal tap only spurred her on to reach her goal.

It was years later that I heard, with much sadness, of Geraldine's untimely death. Struck down with a terminal illness, when she was in her mid-twenties.

That year in Grade 9, a new English teacher, Miss Vigrass, arrived. With a strong English accent, she was the first white teacher at our school. Gentle and softly spoken, blond hair draped over her shoulders, she seemed awkward at first. As the weeks progressed, she engaged us in essay-writing and poetry.

This was when my love of writing started. Eager to please her, I put extra effort into my essays. Most of my stories centred around being lost in a forest and the many challenges in finding my way back. With her encouragement and as my imagination exploded, I developed these tales into magical adventures. Her feedback was always full of praise with further tips on how to build my story.

Her teaching and interest in my writing gave me a sense of pride, something that had been missing since I started high school. I started to write in every spare moment.

When I started menstruating at school, I turned to Frances for help. In the bathroom she rolled off a thick wad of toilet paper for me to line my underwear with. At home, she gave me some of her flannelette strips and that evening she spoke to Mum about us using sanitary towels and that it was also time for me to start wearing a brassiere.

Since starting high school, Frances and I had grown much closer. We shared many secrets about boys at school and listened to records and our favourite radio programmes after school. We followed the serials on Springbok Radio, rushing home every afternoon to listen to the next episode. These stories were all about white families living on farms. *Die Geheim van Nantes* and *Die*

Banneling were Afrikaans soap opera style family tales of love and deception in farm settings that had us spell-bound.

Frances introduced me to many of the American and British pop singers. At the time, her favourite artist, the American soul singer Percy Sledge, had plans to tour South Africa.

'I am going to save up and buy tickets for us to see Percy Sledge when he comes to the Luxurama Theatre,' she told me.

I had only been to the Princess, our local bioscope, once, the time when she took me to see Julie Andrews in *The Sound of Music*. We sang all the songs for weeks and acted out the parts the children played.

I could hardly contain myself when we travelled to the non-white Luxurama Theatre to purchase tickets for the Percy Sledge concert.

'Why are you going to see someone who is selling out the rights of black people?' Dad asked. 'This is not right. He should be banned for agreeing to perform to segregated audiences.'

'I am not going to miss the chance to see Percy Sledge,' Frances said indignantly. 'He may never come again and then I would have missed it.'

Georgie, who did not have money for his ticket, agreed with Dad. 'I am not going,' protested Georgie. 'Why should I support him when he does not support us?'

'So, you are going to travel from our segregated suburb, on a segregated train to a segregated theatre to see a black singer from America,' exclaimed Dad.

But Frances did not care, all she wanted was to see Percy Sledge live on stage singing all our favourite songs.

In May 1970, we waited among screaming fans for Percy Sledge to walk onto the stage, dressed in tight pants and platform shoes. The audience erupted and when the band struck up with the opening song, *My Special Prayer*, I was in awe. It was one thing to listen to a record, but it was a wonderful experience to see the person live on stage.

Everyone cheered, screamed, and clapped for the King of Soul, as he was known to us. Many could not believe that he was right there in South Africa, and at the end of the show, we joined the audience shouting, 'Don't go back Percy, stay here in South Africa.'

Percy Sledge, who was extremely well received, held sold-out concerts around the country. In the Luxurama Theatre, he performed for non-whites, and a short distance away, at The Three Arts in Plumstead, he performed for whites.

On his return to America, Percy Sledge was black-listed by the Actor's Equity for performing to segregated audiences in South Africa.

I found my first part-time job at a clothing shop on Retreat Road. At the interview, Mr Joshlowitz, the Jewish owner, was pleased with my calculation accuracy and hired me on the spot. I worked Friday afternoons and Saturday mornings until 1 pm. My job was to unpack new stock and fill up the drawers and shelves. I also served customers under his watchful eye. My pay of four Rand was handed to Mum.

As was our custom, particularly among coloured people, parents controlled their children's money. Mum would give me 50 cents and kept the rest towards our household budget.

Folding the new underwear and socks and arranging them in different sizes in the drawers was the exciting part of my job. For the first few weekends Mr Josh supervised my work, teaching me how to fold items and to attach the price tags.

Noticing how much I enjoyed unpacking the new stock and arranging them neatly in the drawers he approached me one afternoon, 'You are welcome to lay-by some clothing and I will subtract instalments from your pay.'

I started lay-byes for many different colours and styles of underwear for all of us at home. Whenever it came to the final payment, Mr Joshlowitz would hand me my package without taking the payment.

I worked in the store until I finished my studies.

7

APARTHEID INTENSIFIED

STEENBERG, SOUTH AFRICA: JANUARY 1972, MID-SUMMER

Months before my final exams, I had decided against pursuing a teaching career. The effect of Dad's illness and our cramped conditions had taken its toll. My school work was suffering and I had no desire to pursue further studies.

I would become lost for hours writing, creating little stories, cutting papers into squares, folding them in half and stitching them together with a needle and cotton. I gave these as gifts to Maureen and Andy and the neighbourhood children.

A few years prior, I had joined the international pen-pal network and regularly wrote to a pen-friend in Germany, and Sonia Anderson who lived in Jamaica. Sonia and I wrote to each other weekly for the next ten years and formed a strong bond. Her letters were filled with interesting stories about Kingston town where she lived with her family. At the time, I had no idea that Sonia was black. She described her happy childhood and I tried hard to emulate her stories by writing creative, albeit slightly exaggerated tales about our area and family.

Mum encouraged me to reconsider a teaching career and for a while I wrestled with this option. A coloured primary school teaching course, at the time, required students to hold a minimum Grade 10 qualification. I wanted to be a writer but everyone at home scoffed at that idea. My handmade story books lay around the room until Mum threw them in the bin.

Finally, I relented and went for the medical examination, as required by the education authority at the Department of Coloured Affairs.

'Remove all your clothing, and step on the scale so that I can record your weight and height,' the Doctor said. 'Then I must examine a few other things.'

I stood on the scale, waiting for him to record my weight and measure my height. But staring at my naked body, he remained in his seat, directing me to turn around. Embarrassed, I tried to cover my breasts and pubic area with my hands.

He continued the examination on the bed, listening to my heartbeat, touching my chest between my breasts. With both hands he touched my breasts, and then brushed his hands down my arms and legs. I pushed his hand away and covering my breasts with one arm, I jumped off the bed, grabbed my underwear. With my back turned to him my fingers could not clasp my bra fast enough.

Fully dressed and with clenched fists, I stood waiting

while he calmly completed the form. I felt the heat rise in my cheeks. The silence in the room overwhelmed me and without collecting the form, I rushed towards the door and ran all the way home.

Too humiliated to tell anyone, I tried to forget about the incident. So many thoughts about my studies raced through my mind. *What will I tell Mum? What will I do about my studies?* I knew that Mum would be very disappointed if I did not pursue a teaching career. I had to think of something else to do. Going to university later was not an option unless I was able to get a bursary because Mum could not afford the fees.

That evening, as if through divine intervention, Frances brought home a small typewriter from her workplace. She had recently started evening typing classes at Battswood High School in Wittebome.

'This is how you insert paper,' she demonstrated, holding the paper behind the roller and slowly turning the knob until the paper appeared. 'You should learn to type properly. There is a college in Wynberg, Maurice's Business College, Mum could let you study there full-time.' Looking down at the typewriter, she continued, 'I wish that Mum could have afforded to send me for training before I applied for jobs. I have no office skills and now I have to attend night classes to learn how to type.'

'Will you tell Mum about the college?' I asked, my eyes widened with excitement. 'The money from my part-time job at the shop can pay some of the fees. Please, please,' I begged.

'Ok, Ok, I will ask Mum. But let's wait for the right moment. I will explain that it's best for you to have some office skills before you start working, and Maurice is a good college.'

Maurice's Business College, the first of its kind for non-white students, had opened in 1969 in the suburb of Wynberg. Mrs Maurice, the principal, had great vision and a passion for education. While we were served gutter education by the government, she ensured that her students— or her girls, as she referred to us—would graduate with the skills and knowledge equal to white students.

When Frances broached the subject, Mum wasn't convinced that this would lead to the right job for me. But Frances, feisty as always, put forward a strong case. In the end Mum agreed that I could visit the college to collect the enrolment forms.

Frances, fiercely protective of me, ensured, through keeping her eye on the latest fashion and hairstyles, that we did not lag behind others. Using her sewing skills very early on, she would make identical outfits for the two of us to wear to the youth club or outings. Many times, these outfits were best worn in the dark because finishing was not her strongest skill.

When the first day of college arrived, I travelled on the train to Wynberg, dressed in a green skirt and white blouse. I met Angela, a girl from the neighbourhood, on the station and felt less nervous when she told me that she was on her way to Maurice.

We had so much to talk about and moved along the platform to our designated segregated carriages that had become our way of life. We were just two girls from the council housing estate who could attend this prestigious college for coloured girls. This alone carried a certain status and gave us an opportunity to rise above the menial jobs offered to most coloured women.

Public service jobs in administration were reserved for whites. Banks had started employing coloured tellers but opportunities were limited. Most front-line jobs were given to white employees for fear of white customers' objections to having to deal with a coloured person. Services such as post offices and libraries were limited in our areas which reduced the chances of finding employment locally.

The college was set in an old renovated house. The bedrooms and living areas had been converted into class-rooms. The grounds were filled with trees and offered a tranquil setting. Strict but kind-hearted, Mrs Maurice assisted students where she could with fees, books and even toiletries.

Elegantly dressed in business attire, Mrs Maurice introduced us to the British-developed Pitman's short-hand—at the time a subject taught only at white colleges. Our lessons included personal hygiene and deportment to help us develop confidence and to present ourselves as graduates with skills to match white young women in the business world. The examinations were conducted externally by the Department of Coloured Affairs, which gave us a second-grade but still recognisable qualification.

'Sit up straight and watch your posture,' Mrs Maurice often remarked as she walked past our classrooms. 'Posture is important in the business world and ladies representing this college must make an impression from the moment they step through the front door of any business,' she added.

Most girls were well-groomed, and thankfully I could lay-by clothes at Mr Josh's shop to try and keep up with the way the other girls dressed. When I finally paid my last instalment on a pair of the fashionable La Finesse and V-knee jeans I could not wait to wear them to college. My V-knee jeans, with a V-shape stitched across the fold of the knee, was the very latest trend.

In the afternoons, Dad would dictate to me from the newspapers, and this challenged me to speed up my dictation and increased my ability to decipher more complex words. My skills progressed quickly and soon I could read back my dictation with 100% accuracy.

We learned touch-typing on Everest typewriters with blank keys. With our eyes fixed on a large image of a keyboard on the wall, we listened to the recorded instructions. At the end of the line the voice would say 'carriage return', making us quickly reach for the lever to turn up to the next line.

At the start of the year, Dad had completed my application form for an identification book. Mum, Dad and Frances had green identification cards with the words 'mixed race', identifying as coloured. Georgie was the first one in our family to be issued with the new dark blue identification book.

I arrived home one afternoon to Dad excitedly waving an official brown envelope containing my dark blue identity book. With Dad hovering over me, we stood in the lounge room while I opened the envelope.

'I almost opened it thinking it was addressed to me,' said Dad, who shared the same initial as mine.

Following him to the kitchen table, he explained, 'These thirteen numbers, under the Population Registration Act, classify you as a Cape Coloured. Your identity number starts with the six numbers of your birth date.'

Pointing to the rest of the numbers, he said, 'Now, the next four numbers identify you as female, and these numbers at the end, 01, identify your race as Cape Coloured. White people are identified by the last numbers 00.'

Waving my book in the air, he walked into his bedroom cursing the government.

'This damn shameful government uses these numbers to put you into a racial group.'

In the room he lit a cigarette, and lay on the bed, blowing smoke into the air, coughing and wheezing until I handed him a glass of water.

'Don't ever let this government stop you from doing anything,' he muttered. 'You must work hard. You are smart and will have good qualifications. Remember, no one can take that away from you. Your sister was denied her chance to work in the field that she wanted to do. There is nothing that I, her father, could do about it. Nothing,' he said, pushing his fist onto his chest. 'Do you know what that feels like, to tell your child she is the wrong skin colour? I had to open the letters and read it and then tell her that she cannot ever be a radiographer,' he continued.

I remained next to the bed while Dad coughed and spluttered as he puffed away at his cigarette, reaching to tip his ash into the ashtray next to the bed, but the ash tipped onto the side table.

In my head, I screamed, *Stop smoking Dad, you are going to die. What does it matter if I am a Cape Coloured? So are you. You have the same numbers in your identification book.*

But I could not say that to him. It would have been disrespectful and Dad would have gone off on a tangent to clarify his foreign classification.

Instead, as he coughed, I held the glass closer to his mouth and said, 'It's okay, Dad; here drink your water.'

That winter, Dad spent weeks in bed. Dr Moss's home visits became more frequent and Dad received cortisone injections to open his bronchial pipes. Maureen had started high school and she took on more responsibility helping Dad in the afternoon and taking care of Andy after school, until I arrived home from college.

Because of our cramped home and Dad's alcohol abuse we never invited our friends home. On weekends Georgie and Frances were often out while I spent my time at home with Mum, Dad and Andy. Maureen took refuge at her best friend Pauline's house down our street; she often spent the entire weekend with them.

Over the months, Frances had developed a strained relationship with Dad. She was angered by his reaction in chasing away would-be suitors, especially when he had been drinking.

When she met her first boyfriend, Mum intervened and allowed him to visit her on a Sunday afternoon. Frances spent hours rolling her hair, drying it in the sun and then styled it in a mass of curls bunched up on top of her head.

Mum hung a lace curtain between the hallway and lounge, thick enough to give them privacy but short enough for Frances to see her walk past the living room. As soon as her boyfriend said his goodbyes, I rushed to lay on her bed, waiting to hear all the juicy bits.

Mum tried her best to improve our living standard, and with the addition of Frances's and Georgie's wages she could buy new household items on a hire purchase agreement. We were excited beyond words when our little record player was replaced with a shiny new radiogram with a glass cabinet on the top. The bottom had two sections, with a pull-down door revealing a radio on the one end and a turntable on the other end. That was the start of my love affair with music. I could sit for hours watching how the diamond tip needle connected with my seven single to fill the lounge with music.

In the glass cabinet, on the top shelf, Mum displayed a new dinner service and fancy glasses on the lower shelf.

'This is only to be used for special occasions like Christmas,' Mum said. 'Frances, it will be your job to unpack and clean the glass cabinet once a month.'

In the kitchen, our Jewel wood-fire stove was replaced with a four-plate electric stove. We no longer had the hot water boiler and had to use a big pot to warm our bath water.

The highlight of my week was to attend the youth club at St Mary's parish on a Sunday. This was a chance to have fun, to dance to our favourite music, and to meet our cousins. I struck up a firm friendship with Ronald, a new member, who lived a few streets away from our house.

Ronald, the youngest child in his family, had moved from another area to live with his sister and her family. He was two years ahead of me at school. Reserved and shy at first, he soon blossomed to reveal his true personality, that of a sensitive and caring young man.

We shared deeply about our lives and our interpretation of the scriptures. Religion influenced our lives greatly and we marvelled at the works of our Creator. This soon developed into our special time to bare our souls without fear or ridicule.

'When I listen to the gospel during Mass, I would look for ways to interpret that into my daily life,' he said.

'I don't always understand some of the readings,' I said. 'I just want God to step in and improve our lives. Why is he so absent when there is so much suffering?'

His reasoning was always, 'God cannot do everything. We must look at how the message in the gospel can make us better people and how we can bring about peace for everyone.'

Jokingly I said, 'You have the patience of Job; I think you should become a priest.'

Shrugging off my suggestion, he would tease, 'You are forever the Doubting Thomas. Have faith that our lives will improve.'

Whenever he smiled, his whole face lit up and for a few moments the seriousness of his demeanour would disappear.

Whenever I shared my shame about our overcrowded council house, or my father's drinking, he would remind me of the many positive things around me.

'These challenges are sent to test our faith. It's part of our journey through life,' he reminded me.

Somehow he always found ways to allay my fears about being trapped in poverty forever. To change the mood of our conversation he would direct the conversation to what we both aspired to.

'What is the first thing that you are going to buy when you start working?'

'Definitely a Crosby Stills Nash and Young LP.'

'I would like to save my money to buy my mother a house,' he said. 'She worked so hard all her life and deserves to have her own home.'

While Ronald and I loved dancing, and usually we were the first ones on the dance floor, it was Georgie who was the popular dancer in the youth group. The girls clamoured to dance with him and he loved to do the fashionable dance, the bop, with both Frances and me as his partners. Skilfully he would swing us around, twisting and turning with expert hands and feet.

Georgie also excelled at ballroom dancing. When some of the youth group members took ballroom classes with Manny Gomez, the renowned dance teacher, Georgie mastered the steps with ease. He was a joy to watch as he glided across the floor with elegant grace. He had the skill and personality to make any dance partner feel like a professional dancer.

During this time I also befriended Desmond, another youth club member, who often walked home with us. He invited me to my first coffee bar. Inside these cafés, located in secret underground locations, the smoke hung thickly in the air and people of all colours sat around on the floor or on stools listening to music, smoking joints and drinking alcohol. *Never* any coffee in sight.

At these places, I was introduced to illegal interracial mixing and exposed to the music of British Afro-Pop band Osibisa and Crosby, Stills, Nash and Young. The atmosphere was hushed, and I was attracted to the music and the whole hippy ambience. While I knew it was illegal and that police raids at these places would land me in jail, the music and being in Desmond's company clouded my judgment.

My interest in apartheid intensified when I joined the Young Christian Workers (YCW). This was a world-wide movement, created by Cardinal Joseph Cardjin from Belgium, aimed at improving the living and working conditions of workers. The government was opposed to the YCW because in South Africa, its main aim was to work towards overcoming the injustices of racial segregation.

Dressed in faded jeans, dyed grandpa vests and peace signs, along with youth club members, I joined the crowds at these Young Christian Workers multi-racial rallies. These events were held on church properties and for reasons unbeknown to me, police raids never occurred. We listened to robust speeches centred around the impact apartheid had on workers and the ongoing fight for changes.

This left us, albeit for a short time, stirred and filled with rage about the injustices and to ponder our future in apartheid South Africa.

'We shall overcome, we shall overcome,' we sang boisterously to the sounds of guitars and penny-whistles.

Punching the air and hugging each other, people of all colours reached out to form circles while belting out 'Onward Christian Soldiers' at the top of our voices.

The atmosphere at the rallies was in stark contrast to Mum's reaction at home. Whenever I raised this subject, her response was always the same. Unlike Dad, who regularly cursed the government's divisive policies, Mum brushed it aside.

'I am not sending you to college or church to get arrested and thrown in jail,' she would say. 'Will these people help any of you if that happens? Stop talking to me about people who are stirring up trouble. Keep believing that your freedom will come through a good education and not running around protesting.'

Mum's reaction angered me at times. I could never

understand how she could be so accepting of our fate and why it was not open for discussion. She remained steadfast in her belief that every year brought her closer to her goal and her responsibility of raising and educating us. I realised that her fierce determination, in a near hopeless situation, is what kept us going through those tough years.

'You will thank me one day when you earn good wages and you are able to buy the best things in life. Don't fill your head with wanting to fight the government to bring about change. Fight back with a good education.'

Despite Mum's warning, I continued to attend rallies and my resentment towards her indifference to apartheid grew.

I was now confronted with it everywhere I went.

Once oblivious to segregated living, the daily travel on the train in segregated carriages, signs on benches, separate footbridge to our platform, and separate entrances in public buildings now stared me in the face.

For the most part, these injustices stirred up feelings of anger. I began to identify with Dad's feelings of resentment and frustration and sought his company more and more. When he talked, I listened more intently and contributed to the conversation with my own views about the signs on trains or benches relegating us as inferior to white people.

'Use the white entrances, sit on their benches,' Dad would say mockingly, folding his arms as if to ward off the authorities. 'If they stop you, point to other coloured people and say, 'let them go there.''

Dad's view, after a few years of being confined to the house, was however filled with a blind anger and bitterness. His isolation through ill health and lack of stimulation frustrated him more than apartheid.

Frances, now twenty, and after her short-lived relationship, felt increasingly frustrated with her struggle to meet a boyfriend. She spent many hours fretting about being left on the shelf like an old maid. Georgie, nearly 19 and popular with the opposite sex, was always out partying and paid little attention to what was happening in our country.

Restless and under-stimulated, I resorted to reading and writing in my room. I looked forward to Sundays when I could hang out at the youth club, dance and have long conversations with Ronald on our walk home.

Later that year, our parish priest Father Anthony Pathe, an Englishman, had invited two youth groups from other parishes in Cape Town. One group was from a 'white' parish in Rondebosch and the other from a 'black' parish in the township of Gugulethu. Father Pathe had this grand vision that we could learn to integrate comfortably in a social setting.

Gatherings like this would have been deemed illegal but being under the protection of the Church, the government did little to police it.

That afternoon we played host to these two youth clubs. Our youth leader tried hard to engage the other groups and to encourage us to play games and interact. Awkwardly at first, we played card games, darts and a board game called 'kerm', which is like a mini pool table. When we started playing our familiar dance music, the white group moved further away into their corner.

'Get everyone up on the dance floor,' Father Pathe urged Ronald and me. 'You must be mingling. You are supposed to talk to each other and have fun,' he said throwing his hands in the air.

With the music on full blast, we danced across the floor, waving our arms at everyone to join us. The visitors stared at our dance moves and moved closer together in their respective groups, clearly uncomfortable with what was expected of them. A few of our members joined in.

'Come on, come on, enjoy yourselves,' Father Pathe walked among us, gently pushing us towards each other.

Eventually we succeeded in getting a few onto the dance floor and soon others followed. Father Pathe leaned against the doorway with a beaming smile, looking at what he had helped to create: young people of all racial groups having fun together.

At the end of the evening, while it was deemed a success in integration, it failed to further Father Pathe's wish for this to become a regular gathering. However, the rulebooks had been broken.

Around this time, my cousin Manuel, Manie for short, the son of Mum's brother, received a bursary to study at university. Manie moved from Bredasdorp, a country town, to live on campus and start his studies at the first university for coloured students, the University of the Western Cape. This university was also known as Bush College, because of its location. Most coloured parents viewed Bush College not only as a place of unequal education but also of inferior education.

The other two higher education institutions were the University of Cape Town and Stellenbosch University. UCT, set majestically overlooking the Cape Peninsula, was mainly for English-speaking white students. This university allowed non-white students to study on a special permit. Stellenbosch University, set in the heart of wine farms, was exclusively for Afrikaner students.

Manie and Georgie quickly developed a close bond and he regularly visited our home. It was refreshing to be in his company and listen to him talk about university life.

I had started joining Frances and Georgie on weekend outings. Along with Ronald and other youth club members, we went dancing at our local nightclubs. Popular nightclubs were the Jolly Carp, the Peninsula and the Brothers Club. House parties under tarpaulins, known as 'scenes', were also popular. Entry fees were referred to as 'bread'.

The local sports clubs arranged the annual Mardi Gras at the William Herbert grounds in Wynberg. This was a highly anticipated event on our social calendar. A feast of food stalls, merchandise, theme park and cultural activities, it was held over a weekend. Here I saw my first sword-swallowing 'khalifa' show.

Popular coloured DJ Ely's Coming would take us on a musical journey, and introduced us to strobe lighting. Ely, a DJ of note, worked as a storeman during the day. But at night he donned his trademark hat and imparted his vast musical knowledge which always left us star-struck. He introduced me to what became my most treasured album, *Kafunta* by British singer PP Arnold.

The innocence of my youth was fast disappearing.

Entertainment was restricted to our side of the line on the Cape Flats. On rare occasions, and dependent upon transport, we ventured to other nightclubs, like the Beverly and Goldfinger lounges in other coloured areas. The coloured artists, like pianist Dollar Brand (now an internationally acclaimed artist Abdullah Ibrahim), saxophonists Robbie Jansen and Basil Coetzee, jazz pianist Tony Schilder, Pacific Express, The Rockets and many other non-white bands entertained us with pop and Cape-style jazz.

Many of these coloured artists endured the most inhumane conditions when travelling to performances around the country. There were no hotels or motels for them to sleep in and many resorted to sleeping in their cars. They suffered further humiliation by having to use the bushes on open fields to relieve themselves because they were unable to use toilet facilities at white venues where they performed.

One artist, a renown Cape Town jazz pianist, was forced to play from behind a lace curtain in a venue, so as not to offend the white audience.

Non-white musicians were not afforded radio airplay and these nightclubs were the only places where we could listen to their music. It wasn't until much later that Jonathan Butler became the first non-white local artist to be played on a white South African radio station, with his hit song *Please Stay*—and he earned a Sarie Award, South Africa's equivalent to the Grammy Awards.

On Saturday, 16 September 1972, a chilly Spring morning, I went on an errand for Dad to play his Big Four racing card at the TAB in town. This was a ritual for many coloured people with a dream of a big win on a horse. Dad was no exception. He always just missed a win by one horse filling his trifecta.

That morning I took a shortcut to Retreat Station through Square Hill housing estate, walking past the cottages allocated to non-white railway staff. The tiny cottages lined the street directly opposite the railway line between Retreat and Steenberg stations. Further down, directly across the platform, larger white brick houses lined the footpath. These were allocated to white railway staff. Those were mostly Afrikaner families.

Mounting the steps to the non-white wooden bridge, with the southeaster blowing fiercely, I pulled my green hand knitted scarf tightly around my neck. At the other end of the platform was another bridge for the exclusive use of white residents. After purchasing my ticket at the non-white ticket box, I spotted my friend Robert standing close to the whites-only end of the platform.

Robert, who was engrossed in conversation with a young man dressed in a double-breasted duffle coat, waved at me to come closer. They stood next to the wooden benches marked "Europeans only".

'Meet my friend Christopher Segers,' he said.

Christopher was tall, with dark wavy hair and fair skin. He smiled and reached out to take my hand.

'I am pleased to meet you,' he smiled, then continued his conversation with Robert.

Stealing a quick glance, I noticed the book in his hand, *Fiddler on the Roof*. His thick coat looked expensive with the many gold buttons laid out in a double-breasted formation.

'Where are you heading?' Robert asked.

'I had to get up early this morning to deliver my father's race card to the TAB,' I said, turning my back to the open area to shield myself from the strong wind. 'But it has given me the chance to buy the *Cosmos Factory* album by Creedence Clearwater Revival at the Hippy Market in Long Street.'

Both Robert and Christopher were reserved and

formal. I tried to lighten the atmosphere by telling them about having to get out of bed while everyone else slept at home. We stood talking about our favourite music albums until the train arrived.

The first three carriages, marked for Europeans only, rolled past and we moved closer to the door of the first non-white carriage. The carriages on the back-end, referred to as third-class, were for blacks or non-whites who could not afford second-class. The seats in those carriages were dark-green plastic and positioned around the sides to leave more standing room for the many travellers packed in during peak time.

After Robert had alighted from the train at Claremont Station, Christopher turned his attention to the book. Occasionally he looked up to check which station we were up to. I was instantly attracted to Christopher but he appeared to be more interested in his book.

At Cape Town Station I was surprised when he waited until the guards had checked my ticket. Together we walked towards the non-white exit. Outside, along Darling Street in a fenced-in area, was the Grand Parade, a busy Saturday market. The stalls were filled with a variety of items from flowers to fruit and vegetables, haberdashery and refreshments.

In the hustle and bustle we could hear the hawkers, in the local dialect, doing their utmost to attract customers to their stalls.

'Aartapels en uiwe, tamatie vir die party en uiwe vir die flavour.' 'Appels (apples) en pere (pears), come madam, come nearer,' they sang out in tune.

Cars streamed along Darling Street to the busy intersection at Adderley and Strand Streets. Adderley Street was named after Sir Charles Adderley a British Parliamentarian who played a pivotal role in stopping South Africa from becoming a penal colony.

Nestled in Trafalgar Place, in a lane-way between Strand and Darling Streets, sat the flower sellers. Buckets filled with exotic blossoms spilled along the lane-way. The women pushed for sales of the colourful dyed fynbos, pincushion proteas, carnations, tulips, sweet peas, daffodils, lilies; and my favourite sunflowers, to name a few.

In the backdrop, casting a shadow over Cape Town Gardens, a thick layer of clouds covered the peaks of Table Mountain. At the intersection my eyes scanned the crowd, but Christopher had vanished into thin air.

Needing to get to the TAB before 10 am, I hurried along. Puzzled by his disappearance, I hoped that he would follow me to the TAB.

At the Hippy Market, I browsed through the LPs, before buying *Cosmos Factory*. Weaving in-between the crowds, still hoping to catch another glimpse of Christopher, I made my way back to the station. Pausing outside the shops to look through the glass fronts, I continued the search for him. On the platform, my heart sank. Even though I hardly knew him, I longed to spend more time in his company.

Over the next few months, I worked hard preparing for exams. In the afternoons Dad tested my shorthand by dictating from newspaper articles in *The Cape Times* or *The Cape Argus*. On the kitchen calendar, Mum marked off the days until my final exams.

After a whirlwind of exams and end-of-year parties my last day of college had arrived. It was getting late after a day of celebrations, my train arrived at Retreat Station, at the same time as a train coming from Simonstown, in the other direction.

To avoid the rush of commuters, pushing and shoving on the stairs to cross the bridge, I waited until most passengers had left before climbing the stairs. At the top of the bridge I recognised Christopher in the crowd. He came walking up the stairs from the other platform. Smiling broadly, he signalled for me to wait at the bottom. Kissing me warmly on my cheek, he offered no explanation for his mysterious disappearance the last time we met.

'You must be relieved now that your final exams are behind you. I've just completed my second year as an electrical apprentice, with another two years to go.'

'Yes, very relieved,' I laughed. 'Now I must start job-hunting. My Dad will definitely be scanning the newspapers and circling jobs for me to apply.'

Strolling down the street, we talked and laughed, stopping on the corner for a while. We made no further plans to meet.

'I don't understand this guy,' I told Frances. 'First he disappears without explanation; now he spends an hour talking to me—and makes no plans to meet again.'

'You should have asked him straight out,' she said in her usual feisty manner. 'Who knows, he may already have a girlfriend.'

Refusing to believe that, I continued hoping that I would run into him again.

During the Christmas holidays I joined my siblings and cousins at camp in a suburb called Kommetjie, set high up in the mountains. Kommetjie was a white suburb, but the beach area, Soetwater—which was unsafe for swimming—was a popular camping spot for coloured people.

Lorries filled with families, tents and supplies, including their pets, travelled from all over Cape Town. One family even erected a chicken pen next to their tent to house their chickens.

After spending a few days at camp, soaking up the sun and having a good time, Christopher was furthest from my mind. However, when I returned home on New Year's Day, Mum greeted me with a package in Christmas wrapping.

'A young man driving a fancy car came around looking for you,' Mum said. 'You know, these Hendricks boys and their friends walked around the car inspecting it,' she continued. 'I wish they would pull up their pants and wear a belt.'

I knew immediately who it was and cringed at the thought of the guys next door embarrassing me.

8

A WHITE SOCIETY

At the age of 17 I started my first full-time position as a junior clerk at a building company in Newlands, a beautiful southern suburb for 'whites only'

'You must make sure that your hair is straight,' said Frances. 'White people judge your class by your hair.'

After I tried on a few different outfits, she helped me settle on the one to wear for my first day. That night I knelt next to the kitchen table while she smoothed out parts of my hair, covered it with brown paper and ironed it until all the waves were removed.

On the Cape Flats I was influenced by women who spent hours straightening their hair. Coloured people talked about their white heritage as if it separated them from black people. No one referred to their indigenous ancestors. Just like straight hair and fair skins brought us closer to whites, it also separated us from black people.

It gave us our own classification and allowed us to walk a few steps behind white people. Unlike black people, who could not walk on the same street.

Whites—we had to aspire to be like them to succeed in life.

Ironing hair in the 1960s and early '70s was the *in* thing. In Mum's younger days they used an iron comb, warmed over the flames of a primus stove and pulled through their hair to straighten it. Women with coarse, curly hair massaged it with oil, making the hot iron hiss and smoke to rise as they combed it through.

Most commuters alighting from the train at Newlands coming from my side of the line were coloureds: gardeners, housemaids or a few office workers. The offices of the building company had a perfect view of the majestic Kirstenbosch Mountain Ranges, and the surrounding tree lined streets were filled with spacious houses. The setting made me suck in the air as if it was cleaner than our air. The streets were quiet; no children running around or dogs barking.

Inside the spacious office, my desk was tucked away in a corner close to Mrs Jeram, the office manager. Excited about my job, I devoured the tasks given to me. Despite having passed with 90 wpm typing and 100 wpm Pitman's shorthand, my job was to fold letters and invoices, unpack stationery items, and to keep the office and kitchen tidy.

'I'll show you how to change the ribbon,' said Mrs Jeram. 'This is a very important task and you must watch closely so that you limit the amount of ink stains on your fingers. Your job is vital, everyone will depend on you to find the right stationery and kitchen supplies.'

After about three months, one Friday morning, Mrs Jeram, who never missed a day at work, had been called home because her son was unwell.

'I will need some urgent help today,' the voice behind me said. 'We have a tender deadline at 5 pm today and there is a lot of typing to do. Are you able to help me?' asked the young project officer.

I was surprised that he had addressed me personally. Mrs Jeram always gave me my tasks.

That day I worked furiously, typing large documents while the project manager, about ten years my senior, hovered around checking my work.

'Not one mistake,' he beamed, handing me the final form to complete while he dictated.

Impressed with my work, he praised my accuracy and speed. Uncomfortable with his praise but excited to finally show off my skills, I was in a hurry to get home to share my news with Mum.

It was well after 5 pm when we completed the work and he insisted on driving me home. I quickly declined, not wanting him to see where I lived, but he insisted.

'No, it is the least I can do for your hard work,' he continued. 'And it is Friday night, you should not travel home on the train so late.'

Reluctantly, I got into the car but started plotting my escape. While he chatted, asking questions about my family and my hobbies, I thought of an escape plan before we reached the housing estate.

'My Dad is a teacher and my mother works as a caterer,' the words tumbled out before I could stop myself. He smiled and I felt that I had met his approval.

'Are you happy at work?' he asked.

Not sure how to respond, I hesitated. But before I could answer, he asked me how much I earned.

'70 Rand a month,' I said proudly glancing at him from the corner of my eye.

But he looked straight ahead and went silent for a while. As we entered our suburb, we passed the free-standing homes and I longed to tell him to stop at one of these houses. Several times I asked him to drop me at certain locations, but he insisted on taking me to the door.

He appeared interested in our surroundings, slowing down to look at the houses and questioning me about sporting facilities. It looked like it was the first time he had entered a coloured housing estate.

When we entered the top of our street, it resembled a dark tunnel, the air hung thickly and I felt my breath quickening. Through the closed car windows, I imagined the smell of our area and it nauseated me. Very different to Newlands.

Our street, a thoroughfare into the housing estate, was always busy with children running around, playing street games. It felt as if the mountains had moved closer, casting a dark shadow over our house and the rest of the street.

Moving around nervously I had hoped that my street would be quiet and the neighbours all inside their homes. But it was Friday night, pay day for everyone; the street was abuzz and inside these homes would be steaks and sausages cooking in frying pans for dinner.

Mothers would have returned from their husband's workplace where they waited to collect their pay before the men headed for the hotel. At this time, some fathers would stagger home drunk and mothers would be preparing to feed their families. It was the day that the account at the corner-shop was squared up and groceries delivered again.

Pure wishful thinking on my part that the street would be quiet.

I kept my eyes peeled to my side of the street and prayed that the Hendricks boys and their friends would not be around. Spotting them at their gate I wanted the earth to open up and swallow me whole. I wished that the council had not opened up the road to extend it across the ravine. I would have preferred to walk across the thin pipe than face the chaos outside our house.

'Further down,' I murmured.

'Hey Beryl, is that your new boyfriend?' I heard one of the Hendricks boys call out.

Walking closer to the car, he cupped his hands on the window to have a look inside the car.

'Thank you,' I mumbled, reaching for the door handle ready to jump out.

Mortified at the sight of the drunken Hendricks boys, and their friends, I raced inside, not waiting for his car to leave.

For a long while, I laid curled up on my bed, tears streaming down my face. All I could think about was that my reputation would be ruined. I desperately wanted to be seen as an educated person, and not as a lowly coloured person from the council housing estate. I felt my carefully crafted image was unravelling. My straight long hair meant nothing. I was still the second-class citizen no matter how hard I tried to be like *them*. *Why did I lie about my parents and the kind of work they did?*

The Cape Flats, the area that the government forced us into, removed our choices, offered us so much less than white people had and could afford. My colleague showed me no disrespect. But, deep inside, my soul wept at this injustice served on our people. For many living in these housing estates, their lives had become a stagnant circle of life. One with little hope of improving.

Our community, forever held back by the colour of our skin, continued to forge a life for themselves. Most people had no chance of reaching their potential. But they carried on living. Some barely existing. This injustice infuriated me.

In my confusion, I resented my parents for being who they are. Consumed with embarrassment, my anger rose towards Mum and Dad for not providing us with a better home. *Why were they born with the wrong skin colour resulting in them having such menial jobs?* All my life we lived in this crammed environment.

Mum's efforts and her struggle all the years to keep a roof over our heads and to maintain the house had been momentarily forgotten. When I heard the front door open, I pretended to be asleep. In the dark room I listened to Mum's movements, pushing her bicycle to the backyard and then filling the kettle. I had no desire to talk to anyone, the excitement and my achievement overshadowed by my embarrassment of our humble surroundings.

A home that I would later long for as my safe-haven, the home that held all our happy memories, and where Owen's faded photo stood on the half-moon table.

That Sunday at the youth group, I tried to shake this heavy feeling. On our way home, I poured my heart out to Ronald. Listening intently until I had finished, he stopped and we sat down on the pavement.

'I know it's hard and I am faced with the same thing many times. But try not to ever let anyone do that to you. White people are human beings just like us,' he admonished me. 'They may think that they are in charge. But you are smart and beautiful. You can do the job. Where you live does not define you.'

We sat talking on the pavement for a long while. As usual he had the knack of making me feel better about myself by focussing on my strengths.

The next morning, I brushed out my swirled hair. It was now the latest method of straightening our hair by twirling it around our heads and covering it with a nylon stocking while we slept. The cap, usually ripped stockings, had been cut off and tied at the top. It was a skilful task, one that required the stocking to be twirled properly, otherwise the top part of the hair would pop out. Great care was taken to keep it off our foreheads; if the stocking was too tight it would leave a red welt across the forehead. That would be a sure sign that our hair was not really straight but had to be straightened.

My long hair was my pride. It gave me a connection to Dad and made me feel closer to his heritage—that of a foreigner, as he never failed to remind us.

About an hour after arriving at work, Mrs Jeram called me to the boss's office. Panicked, my first thought was that I would lose my job. So many thoughts raced through my mind as I stood at the door. *Did it have anything to do with where I lived?*

Inside the office, face-to-face with the boss and the project manager, I glanced at Mrs Jeram standing near the window. Her expression dark and unfriendly.

'Well done on the great work you did on Friday,' said the boss. 'We want to reward you and your pay will now increase to 90 Rand per month,' I heard him say.

I felt the heat rise in my cheeks. Mrs Jeram stood stony-faced and the project manager smiled broadly.

'Thank you,' I said softly before heading for the door.

In the bathroom, staring at myself in the mirror, tears welled up and I cried softly with relief. Splashing my face with water, then patting it dry with toilet paper I walked back to my desk.

'Get back to work,' said Mrs Jeram in her icy tone. She was clearly upset that my plight had progressed to the highest level without her input.

But my heart sang with joy. That evening I rushed home to share the exciting news with Mum.

Sitting on the couch, a beaming smile lit up her face, in her lap her hands clasped as if in prayer. She said, 'I knew you would be good at your job.'

I knew then that she was so proud of me.

But a restlessness had surfaced in my thoughts. I was more conscious of our surroundings. I had grown up oblivious to the signs on trains and benches. Without flinching I would use the correct entrance at the post office or bank.

Until now. Now everything felt different.

That August, there was much excitement as Frances celebrated her twenty-first birthday with a big party. Mr Freedberg, Dad's old boss, supplied the alcohol for the celebration. Mum had booked St Mary's Hall and some of her friends helped to prepare the catering and decorating. Dad was up out of bed and smartly dressed, wearing his favourite braces for the occasion.

It was the biggest party in our entire family, and Mum had planned every detail. A popular live band had people dancing all night and the well-stocked bar was a highlight. This was the occasion that Mum had been saving for.

'Twenty-one and unattached,' said Mr Dreyer at the end of his speech. However, there were no suitors at the party to take up the role.

Georgie, who was in his third year as an apprentice, showed off his carpentry skills by building an enclosure around the square cement patch outside the back door. Complete with a roof and cladding, this added an additional room to the house, giving us more space to turn it into a bedroom for Georgie. As a surprise to me, he built a bookshelf in our bedroom to store my many books.

'Now, I have a place to display my plants,' Mum said excitedly as she surveyed the corner of the new room.

After Frances's birthday celebrations, Dad went back to spending most days in bed. Mum had finally left the bakery and started working at a restaurant in Wetton, close to the place where she bought her first bicycle back in 1964. Frances had started saving to buy her first car, a white Volkswagen Beetle.

9

CHRISTOPHER

SOUTH AFRICA: AUGUST 1973, EARLY SPRING

As I was leaving the local dentist surgery, I bumped into Christopher on his way home from work. This time it was a joyous meeting. We laughed and talked for hours and agreed to meet on the Saturday to see a movie.

'It's by time,' Frances quipped. 'Tell him, time waits for no man. He can't expect you to wait around forever.'

'Where is this guy from? He needs a bomb under his backside, if you ask me,' said Georgie.

When Christopher turned up to collect me in his father's shiny green Valiant, some or our neighbours watched as he opened the door for me. Keeping my head down I tried to ignore the comments of the Hendricks boys.

'Beryl, is this one your new boyfriend?' one of them called out.

'Fancy car for a fancy boy,' called out another guy who lived down the road.

'Don't worry, Mrs Crosher, I told him that he must look after her,' Jeffery said when he spotted Mum at the gate.

'Hey, Mister, we are watching you; this girl is like my sister, so make sure you bring her back safely,' said Jeffrey.

Trying to hide my smile, I looked the other way.

Our first date was to our local bioscope, the Princess Theatre on Retreat Road, right across from Mr Josh's shop where I worked during my student years. A stately theatre in the early years, the Princess was next door to the Retreat Hotel where the ladies from our area danced on a Saturday night. People usually dressed up for evening shows. In the ticket box sat Mrs Gaby, and Bassa, the flamboyant doorman, welcomed patrons, often pulling spare tickets out from under his hat for favoured customers.

After our first date, Christopher became a regular visitor in our home. We spent hours getting to know each other. I stopped going to the youth club and saw Ronald only occasionally. He was in a new relationship and whenever we saw each other our conversations were limited to our new relationships. Because Christopher had a car, Mum and Dad allowed me to go out with him over the weekends. We discovered a shared love of music and he introduced me to the movies. Long debates and discussions often ensued after the movies. He was the only person I knew who subscribed to the British film magazine *Photoplay*.

'I was adopted at five days,' he blurted out during one of our conversations. 'I have met my birth mother but we've never spoken about the adoption. One day I will tell you more about it.'

One of the first places he showed me was his childhood home at No. 3 Hanover Street, Diep River. At the age of 12, during his last year in primary school, he arrived home and found his distraught mother sitting on their furniture outside the house. She had made him a sandwich on their kitchen dresser while he sat confused on a chair under a tree on the pavement.

'I had no idea what was happening. My father worked away for the week in Saldanha Bay, at the army base, and came home Friday afternoons, so he was not around to help.'

'My father would have cursed if they did that to us. What did you do? Did they break your stuff? I heard that some people complained about the way their belongings were dumped on the pavement.'

'I sat watching the workers knocking boards up over the windows and doors. There was nothing I could do,' he said.

A family friend had helped his mother to get back into their home after the council discovered that they were one of a handful of families who owned their home and were not renters.

'My parents were given a reprieve of three months to sell the property and move out. It was then sold to a builder for a pittance of the value of the home,' Christopher said sadly.

Tenderly, I asked, 'How did you feel, when you had to move out?'

'I thought of my father,' he said. 'Everything he worked so hard for had to be given away. He loved the backyard and whenever he was home, that's where we would find him, working away on something for the house. Our lives changed dramatically. Moving to Retreat meant that instead of walking to school, at South Peninsula High, I now had to cycle, or use public transport. It was a big adjustment and we were separated from our neighbours and all our conveniences.'

'A few families living in our area were also forcibly removed from Diep River and nearby Steurhof. It's so wrong and degrading to non-white people, that white people can have the power over us,' I lamented.

'What really gets to me is that everyone just moved on with life and accepted this treatment. If we speak up or oppose the government they can lock us up,' Christopher said, getting heated. 'All my childhood friends have been scattered around the Cape Flats and I've lost contact with them. Many families ended up living in squalid conditions in concrete jungles, blocks of flats far away from places of employment and their usual amenities.'

I sensed the pain he felt when he stood outside the fence of the park in which he had once played as a child but now could no longer enter.

Every evening after dinner, Christopher arrived at our home with a pile of LPs, many of them soundtracks to his favourite movies. Often he'd surprise me with my favourite, Cadbury's Whole Nut chocolate, and we would spend the time together in the lounge listening to music on our radiogram.

As an only child, he enjoyed the hustle and bustle of our family home.

'Your parents are always in their bedroom when I come over. My mother would have been sitting with us in the lounge,' he laughed.

Dad's dreaded cough was the only thing we would hear during the evening. Frances often remained in the room reading but many times we would all sit around listening to the music. The house was so small that conversations could be heard no matter where you were.

Maureen and Andy loved the luxuries that Christopher brought for them most nights. Usually around 9.30 pm Dad called out that it was time for us to go to bed. It puzzled me that Christopher preferred to spend so much time at our small house instead of their big house where he had his own bedroom, a record player and a piano. They even had a spare bedroom for visitors.

That winter of 1974 was particularly cold, and Dad's asthma was at its worst. He had stopped smoking and drinking a few weeks prior. Battling his severe coughing, the sound of his chest's wheezing could be heard throughout the house.

Frustrated with his ailing health he resorted to spending his day, when he was not drinking, doing crossword puzzles and listening to the radio. On the calendar in the kitchen, Dad had marked the dates of the much-anticipated rugby tour of the British Lions between May and July 1974. He had still not recovered from the Lions' loss to the all-white Springbok team in 1968 and wanted them to extract revenge this time.

Many evenings I would sit talking to him at his bedside to keep him company. I feared mostly that he would choke during one of his coughing bouts.

'Don't knit so fast, you are making it harder for me to breathe when you move your arms,' he would say to me in-between breaths.

10

GOODBYE DAD

HOME, SOUTH AFRICA: JULY 1974, MID-WINTER

During the second week in July we were all struck down with a severe influenza. Mum cooked pots of soup to keep us nourished while we spent our days in bed recovering. On the morning of 12 July, it was pay day for Georgie and he felt well enough to go to work. Dad's breathing had become extremely laboured and he hardly spoke. While Mum hung the blankets on the line to air in the winter sun, we sat in the backyard to get some sun and fresh air.

'Ben, you must get back to bed,' I heard Mum say.

At the back-door, fully dressed, Dad stood in the doorway. His unruly curly locks hung over his forehead. He looked at us for a few minutes and smiled weakly before turning around back to bed.

We continued sitting outside for a while until Mum

took the blankets back inside.

'Frances, Beryl, come quickly,' she called out. 'I can't hear your father breathing. It's so quiet.'

We rushed inside to his bedside. Frances felt his pulse and listened for his heartbeat, then she looked at us and nodded at Mum. Mum cried softly and we huddled together next to the bed in silence. I stood looking at Dad; he looked at peace. His eyes gently closed, unruly curls framing his face, his heavy breathing silenced. Next to the bed stood his tablets and his Ventolin puffer.

I called Georgie at work, and his boss sent him home immediately with a driver. When he arrived home, he knelt at Dad's bedside and sobbed until Mum moved him away. Mr Oliver, who lived next door, helped Mum wash Dad's body before the undertakers arrived. Mum decided to dress Dad in the new pyjamas I had given him for Father's Day. *The winter pyjamas should keep him warm,* I thought.

On Monday 15 July 1974, Dad's 60th birthday, we laid him to rest. Christopher attended Dad's funeral and stood next to me at the graveside. I thought of Owen, whose burial spot was on the other side. Thirteen years ago, he was buried in this same graveyard. I was just a little girl then when they lowered his small white coffin down the hole.

As Dad's coffin lowered into the ground, I moved closer and stood on the fake grass mat to watch the straps slowly release the coffin down the hole.

'Happy 60th Birthday, Dad,' I said, releasing a handful of flowers on the coffin.

After the funeral, family and friends gathered at our house for the wake. I could not bear the laughter and gaiety of family and friends celebrating Dad's life. Most of them had never spoken to Dad or knew what he believed in. They didn't know him the way we did. He might have been a dreamer and a sickly man but he was passionate about many things. Here they were drinking alcohol, talking and laughing as if they knew him.

Maureen had disappeared to her friend down the road. I stood around for a while watching Andy wandering around the house, sitting on Mum and Dad's bed or walking in the backyard. While we all coped with Dad's death in different ways, Andy, who was just ten years old, looked lost and no one took the time to comfort him and explain the changes Dad's death would bring to daily life. Instead of coming home after school, he now had to wait at Mrs Oliver's house until Maureen arrived home from high school.

The previous few days had been like a whirlwind, Frances and George took charge of the funeral arrangements. They both became overwhelmed when they had to choose Dad's coffin at the funeral undertakers. Frances's relationship with Dad had not been that great in recent years and she remained embarrassed and angry at him for his constant drinking.

When Christopher went home I could not join the jubilant wake. Still dressed in my navy-blue dress I decided to walk to Ronald's house. I wanted to talk to someone about Dad being gone, to cry and say how much I wanted him back. Life felt different now, the house was not the same. A wave of sadness hit me as I walked down the road. Looking down at my shoes I tried to hide the tears from people walking past as I hurried along towards Ronald's house.

I found some comfort with him and his Mum. I didn't have to explain why I was there. They welcomed me inside and we sat drinking tea until he walked me back home.

I missed my chats with Dad. He had fire in his soul but had lost his way during the turbulent times. Like many men of his ilk, he had felt a sense of helplessness and that the odds were stacked against him. Some of these men were strong enough to plod along while others succumbed to alcohol abuse as an escape.

Dad had died the day before the third test of the 1974 British Lions tour of South Africa. He would never know that his beloved Lions team thrashed the all-white Springboks, winning the series by three games and drawing the final test. Georgie and I listened to the third test match in honour of Dad.

Two months after Dad's passing Mum received a letter and 75 Rand from Dad's former boss Mr Freedberg. Georgie, a third-year apprentice carpenter, was saving to buy a car and begged Mum for money to buy my Uncle Kelly's Zephyr.

'Uncle Kelly will sell me his old car for 75 Rand and I will pay back every cent,' Georgie promised. 'Just think, I can drive Mum to the shops and take everyone out,' he went on and on.

Finally, Mum relented and Georgie excitedly set off on foot to my uncle's house to purchase the car. A few hours later we heard what sounded like gunshots outside. In front of our gate, Georgie pulled up in a cream-and-orange coloured Zephyr. Shaking, rattling and backfiring, the car came to a standstill. Beaming from ear to ear, Georgie motioned excitedly for us to come closer.

'I shall christen her Betsy,' he smiled.

Mum declined his offer to take her for a drive around the block. That afternoon Georgie offered to take me for a drive, on condition that I pay for the alcohol. Betsy spluttered and backfired along with the hooter sounding every time we took a right turn down our narrow streets. To my horror, he pulled into a drive-in shebeen, an illegal drinking house, in 7th Avenue, Retreat. Betsy backfired in the drive-way. These shebeens, ordinary houses, had secret serving hatches and some owners went to great lengths to bury their merchandise in case of police raids.

'Hey, you, take that car out into the street,' shouted a man running down the path towards us.

Waving at Georgie to switch off the car, some other men came out to help push Betsy out onto the street. After I bought a bottle of brandy, they push-started Betsy down the road while I remained in the car with my face hidden.

Later that night, on the drive back home, Georgie was unusually quiet, Betsy spluttered and choked all the way, finally switching off at the top of our street. The Hendricks boys came running towards us and helped to push it home. When Betsy mounted the kerb to enter our side driveway Georgie knew that she would never drive on any road again. Betsy remained in the driveway for a few months until Mum asked a junk collector to take it away.

My relationship with Chris had progressed. I hardly went out with my other friends, preferring to spend all my spare time in his company.

On his nineteenth birthday in January, his parents gave him a 1968 white Ford Cortina. He took me on drives around the Cape Peninsula, through suburbs like Sea Point, Camps Bay, Clifton, Llandudno, and all along the coast to Cape Point. This made me *more* aware of how privileged white people were. Luxurious homes with spectacular ocean views were nestled at the foot of the mountains.

It was another world away from the rows of council houses and narrow roads where we were forced to live.

'This is where I work,' he pointed out to the Simonstown Naval Base.

'Oh, you are a sailor,' I giggled.

'No, actually, I am one of six coloured electrical apprentices, in the Dockyard. Engineering and electrical trades were previously reserved for white apprentices only,' he rolled his eyes.

During these drives we could not stop to eat at the cafés or restaurants because they were reserved for white people only. Some of the smaller cafés had a side window through which they would serve non-whites.

Driving along the main road in Simonstown, Chris stopped at the local 'babbie', a term given to Indian shopkeepers.

'When the government's Group Areas Act swept through this area, the Malay shopkeepers could continue trading because they provided a service to the community,' he explained. 'Special concessions were made for them to live in their homes because their businesses were on the same property. But they could not open any new businesses and Malay doctors had to practice in non-white areas.'

As we drove around the area, I understood why the government forcibly removed non-whites. Framed by the majestic mountain ranges with the ocean lapping the sands below, these were picturesque locations, giving the white community access to valuable property and spectacular views.

The removal of non-whites to an area called Ocean View was met with much distress by those affected. Located in a valley, it was impossible to view the ocean, as the name falsely implied. There non-white people were clumped into a housing estate.

Again, families and neighbours were separated, with some having to move to where housing was available. Workers who could once walk or cycle to work now had to travel long distances.

All around us the pain and suffering on our people were immense. We were shunned and pushed into the sand hills and concrete jungles. The cries of the older people were swept up by the wind and carried into the ocean or smashed into the mountain. No one listened.

'When I sit in the train on my way home I enjoy looking at the beach,' Christopher said. 'All the beaches along this railway are for white people. Except for Kalk Bay harbour where the coloured fishermen live in one section. Then from St James, the very next station to Muizenberg, it's for whites only. One of the things I would like to do is walk along the promenade at Fish Hoek.'

'It will never happen in our life time,' I said.

'No, one day I will do that,' he said, his voice trailing off as he looked across the ocean.

'How crazy these laws are,' I said. 'They've taken all the best parts and gave us the worst. Unsafe beaches, housing in low-laying, flood-prone areas, set back into the sand hills. Look at all this, lush green trees, surrounded by water views.'

On these drives we explored many other eating places where we could go to in our own areas, mainly the Cape Flats. I enjoyed the delicious food at the popular take-away café Golden Spoon in Athlone, and the Altona café in Rosmead Avenue was known for the best salomies.

Streetwise and knowledgeable, Chris introduced me to a variety of food at non-white cafes and the few restaurants. One of our favourite places to go after the movies was Cosy Corner, a renowned restaurant catering for coloureds. Owned by a Muslim family, the food portions were huge. My favourite dish was the masala steak and chips served on a large wooden board.

I realised how much living in the housing estate had deprived me of seeing the full scale of the inequality around me. I had lived blissfully unaware of the luxury white people had in the same city I grew up in. This is what the government and the people who voted for them had intended for us. Not just to live separately but to be deprived and to not be good enough to live in the same areas, eat in the same cafes, or sit together in a classroom.

In town, Chris took me to the only coloured restaurant there, the La Fiesta. Eating in restaurants was a new experience for me and one I relished and quickly became very comfortable with.

Chris knew all the secret locations where they screened banned movies and we would join others to watch movies like *To Sir With Love*, *Blazing Saddles*, *A Clockwork Orange*, and *Zulu*. These movies were banned by the apartheid government because they depicted intimate relationships between black and white. The movie *Zulu*, screened to whites only in segregated cinemas, was banned because it showed the uprising of the Zulus.

The thrill of attending those illegal movie screenings, where I met activists and others who openly condemned apartheid, was exhilarating. It aroused feelings of defiance at the injustices meted out to us.

I had become hooked on Chris's *Photoplay* magazine as a source of information about upcoming movie releases. Chris was an avid James Bond fan, so we awaited the first appearance of Roger Moore, our favourite British actor, as James Bond with much excitement.

Chris knew that this James Bond film, *Live and Let Die*, released in early 1973, had departed from the conventional Bond movie plots. This film was set in the African-American cultural centres of Harlem and New Orleans, and the Caribbean Islands.

Live and Let Die marked several milestones, including the appearance of the first romantically involved African-American Bond girl. When the film was first released in South Africa, the love scenes between African-American actor Gloria Hendry and Roger Moore were removed because under the Immorality Act, interracial relationships were prohibited by the apartheid government.

The film was later released on 16mm film and Chris was keen to hire the film for home screening. Much to his dismay the uncensored film was available for hire only to white people.

'This government is going to such great lengths to keep us in the dark,' he said while we sat in the car around the corner from the video store.

'As my Dad would say, they are trying to control our brains,' I laughed. 'Look at your skin, it's whiter than mine and we are mixing.'

But undeterred he had devised a plan to get his hands on a copy of the film by asking a white colleague to hire it on his behalf while we sat a distance away.

These moments of frustration usually passed and we would just get on with life. We were fighting a battle we could not win. But we could strengthen our resolve not to let them extinguish the fire in our souls.

These same feelings of frustration would surface at the Young Christian Workers gatherings. I listened to conversations about Nelson Mandela, who was locked up for treason, and learned about the banned African National Congress. Our level of political discussion at home had been limited to Dad's outbursts and Mum silencing him.

'Sometimes I think we will never be free,' I said to Chris. 'How can we fight this government? They are in control and we are nothing but pawns that they can move around any way it suits them.'

'Yes, I know, but things will have to change, eventually,' was always Chris's answer.

In celebration of the anniversary of our very first meeting, Chris took me to the Gem bioscope in Woodstock. After the movie we bought salomies, a curry-filled roti, a cream soda for me and an iron brew for him. Driving along De Waal Drive he pulled off the road and parked on the side facing the Peninsula. It was a sight to behold; thousands of lights as far as the eye could see. Behind us was the Devil's Peak mountain range.

Promising to show me an even more spectacular sight, he drove further up a narrow dark road towards the mountain, just below the monument of the late tycoon, colonialist and politician Cecil John Rhodes. Rhodes had owned vast areas of the land along the mountain ranges.

On a portion of land he donated, the prestigious white University of Cape Town was built.

In the dark, Chris manoeuvred the car further along the narrow road until we pulled into what looked like a parking lot. As soon as the car stopped, he leaned over to kiss me. I felt his hand searching down the front of my blouse.

'Where is the monument?' I giggled.

But soon the windows had misted over and thoughts of the monument dismissed as I laid in his arms. While we kissed, and giggled, his fingers opened the buttons of my blouse. Suddenly there was a loud bang on our door.

'Make yourselves decent and open this door,' a booming voice commanded.

I recognised the heavy Afrikaner accent. Someone was tugging at my door. I froze.

'Get out now,' he ordered.

Fumbling, I quickly tried to button my blouse. Outside bright lights lit up the area.

Chris whispered, 'It's the police, just do what they say, it will be fine.'

Blinded by the torch light shining directly in my face, a policeman pulled me out of the car. I tried to straighten my clothes and tidy my hair as my feet searched for the ground. Standing face to face with a policeman, my heart raced. I thought about Mum and her fears of us being arrested and thrown in jail.

They could arrest us for being on land owned by white people. But they were looking for something else: couples breaking the law according to the Immorality Act of 1950. One of the most demeaning laws of apartheid, it legislated control over whom we could marry or have intimate relations with. This gave the police the power to vilify citizens if they suspected any intimacy between the races.

Satisfied that we were both coloured, they moved on to the other cars. Chris placed his arm around me, reassuring me that we would be cautioned but not arrested.

As the police pulled people out of the cars, I heard the screams and voices cursing into the night. Describing us as 'hotnots', a degrading term Afrikaners used for coloured people, they had moved to surround a car further down. A woman's piercing screams echoed over the mountains as they dragged her to a police van.

In the moonlight, I saw the light-coloured hair and pale skin of the man, flanked by policemen, walking over to one of the police vans. He climbed into the front seat. The woman, dark-haired and brown-skinned, desperately tried to cover herself as they dragged her across the ground. Someone tried to hand her a jacket to cover herself.

'Be quiet,' the Afrikaner voice ordered as the woman whimpered.

It felt surreal. We could only stand by and watch as this scene played out. These police officers were enforcing the law, the government's Immorality Act, and they relished in their task with an aura of evil. They had the authority to physically abuse the woman because she was non-white, but the man who also broke the law under the Immorality Act sat in the front of the other van. More arrests were made in the darkness below the statue of Cecil John Rhodes.

After the arrests were made we could leave the area. Driving down the narrow path, the noise of the other cars following us filled the air. Chris reached for my hand, rubbing my arm reassuringly. But my mind was on the fate of the young woman. Her screams echoed in my ears. The force, the brutality and the humiliation she endured! One moment she sat quietly in a car with her lover, and in an instant she was publicly humiliated and hauled to the back of a police van.

Shaken and distraught I laid in my bed playing the scenes over in my head. *How could this government continue to treat us like second class citizens?* I could not discuss it with Mum or my siblings because I knew it would greatly curtail my freedom.

The police were particularly drawn to non-white areas and prowled the streets stopping at fancy cars parked in front of our houses late at night. Using their power, they tried to intimidate us, showing us who was in charge. The realities of apartheid manifested clearer in daily life. However, my resolve grew stronger, the fear of being arrested was replaced with a sense of defiance.

When a similar incident happened again in front of our house one night around midnight, I calmly took my time to open the window to let them see our faces. I knew that we weren't breaking *their* law; we were parked in front of *our* house, in *our* street, saying *our* hour-long goodbyes with the car windows misted.

Our conversations became more politically intense and every day injustices led to in-depth discussions and debates. I went from being a naïve girl in the housing estate to becoming street-wise, opinionated and adventurous. Chris always had stories to share about the rife discrimination in the Dockyard and the inferior treatment of blacks. As a non-white apprentice, he had to attend a separate college to his white counterparts.

The things that I took for granted and accepted as our way of life now stared me in the face and angered me. My subservient manner became hardened and daring. I missed Dad, because *now* we could have debated, and I regretted all the times when he talked and I had not paid him much attention.

Now, no longer apprehensive about going to unknown locations to watch banned movies, I felt part of the secret sect, a group of people where the word spread by mouth. We would park our cars away from the house, so as to not attract attention, and casually walk to the location.

While Dad's death was inevitable, his passing shook the bedrock of my life. I missed seeing him lay in his bed or chatting to him in the evenings after work. I tried hard to focus and to keep my mind on daily routine, but I became resentful towards Mum and my siblings who seemed to carry on with living as if Dad had never existed.

After the rush of family and friends who visited our home had subsided, Mum started to remove all traces of Dad's existence: his medication on the dressing table, his clothing. She even replaced their double-bed with two three-quarter beds. That was the final memory of his presence in the room.

For weeks, I played the scene at the funeral service over and over in my head. It was Mum's moment. Something she had been deprived of for many years by the laws of the Church was now possible. For the first time in her 21 years of marriage to Dad, she could receive Holy Communion. I stood behind her as we lined up facing Dad's coffin.

'The Body of Christ,' Father Pathe said to her as he placed his hand on her shoulder for a moment. Before receiving the host, Mum was shaking, her voice barely audible as she whispered, 'Amen.'

Bowing her head over the coffin, she walked back towards her seat, dabbing her tears with a handkerchief. Dad, who had been married briefly before he met Mum, had to first die before she could receive the full sacraments as a widow.

As the shock of his death began to wear off, the full loss of his presence intensified. Even though he had spent most of the past year in bed, he had always been around, and through that my bond with him had remained strong. Although Dad had lost interest in politics and hardly read the newspapers and no longer filled in the crossword puzzle, he never lost his passion for sport.

Saturday evenings had been my most special time with Mum and Dad. That was when we discussed sport and politics, and when I had English vocabulary challenge tests with Dad. On those nights, he was somewhat willing to impart some of his memories of growing up on St Helena, but most times he brushed aside my probing questions about his family and early life. It appeared too painful for him to recall.

A few months after Dad died, we celebrated Georgie's twenty-first birthday with a big party at home. He had recently qualified as a carpenter, and for the first time I saw Mum shed tears of joy. So much had happened to us that year. Frances was now the proud owner of a white Volkswagen Beetle. Kleyweg Bakery, where Mum had worked for many years, had closed and Mum found another job at a restaurant in a suburb called Wetton.

She no longer cycled to work but travelled by train every morning.

To fill the empty void that Dad's passing left in me, I went out more regularly with Chris, and soon we started spending every possible moment together.

The drives around the peninsula unsettled me the most. Being exposed to the luxury that the white people were able to surround themselves with frustrated me. I was envious of this splendour, the beautiful beaches, and many restaurants and cafes for their exclusive use. Cafés and restaurants where we had to be served through a small window while they dined inside with their families. This was so wrong, so inhumane and so degrading to us.

11

SEGREGATED LIFE

My thirst for knowledge about the government and how its apartheid laws had restricted us consumed my thoughts. All the things Dad had said over the years about the government, and the effect it had on our lives, mulled around in my head. It was as though an awakening of my spirit just happened.

But now I thought, *what made white people think that they are better than me? How did our parents and grandparents allow this to happen to them and then in turn to us? This vicious cycle, will continue and our children will be next. They will be seen as inferior to the next generation of white children. When will this end?*

I was thinking about Mum's struggle to provide for us, despite the mighty hand of the law dictating our existence at every turn. This made me realise that she had *no* choices. I accepted that Mum encountered a daily battle to survive in these tough conditions and conceded that she tried her best to prepare for a better future for us than they had.

I now put the blame for our second-class status squarely on the government and its fervent supporters: the white voters. Their unfailing support of the government's policies made it impossible for us to have a say in our own future. They voted and *they* were allowed to shape everything about our lives. With a flick of a pen on a ballot paper, they confirmed their status as the superior race.

More and more I found myself expressing some of Dad's views against the government.

'My dad always spoke about lost opportunities and condemned the power the whites had over us. I am sure if he was a stronger man he would have joined the revolution,' I told Chris.

'That's really all he could do. As much as we hate what's going on around us, there is nothing that we can do to change it,' Chris said. 'Every day I see the injustices meted out to us in the dockyard, but we are powerless to stop it. Someday there may be an uprising, but it will take pressure from the rest of the world to break down apartheid.'

The crowded conditions in our housing estate and the lack of amenities were evidence that segregation was the main reason why our communities did not thrive. We had one public swimming pool, a single small tennis court to serve tens of thousands of residents. How could we possibly succeed?

My siblings and I were some of the fortunate children, bolstered by Mum's belief that education would liberate us. This now started to resonate with me.

One morning, as I climbed the non-white bridge at our station and walked towards the non-white bench to wait for the train, it suddenly dawned on me that we were trapped in this existence. I would never be able to use the other bridge or sit on the seat of my choice. I could only sit there on my allocated non-white bench and watch the first few carriages roll by until the sign said non-whites only. That was my carriage. That is what the law dictated.

I had been so busy growing up that I never noticed or adequately expressed my disgust about the inequality that had manifested itself. I had moments of frustration about our fate but carried on regardless.

Now, I was 19, a woman, and for the first time I felt as if the veil had been lifted. That I could now clearly see these injustices. It unsettled me that Mum grew up like this, and now I was living that same life. I had a better job but my life was still the same. Controlled by a minority group who had the power.

I walked through the non-white entrance and sat on the non-white bench. That was what was expected of me as an obedient citizen: to follow the signs that the government had laid out to rule my life with.

Looking around me, on the crowded platform, non-white people stood around, seemingly oblivious to the discrimination. Even though there were empty benches, they would stand near them while waiting for the train. The signs forbade them to sit down.

My anger rose, I wanted to grab people by the hand and pull them towards the empty benches marked 'whites-only' and scream at them, *Sit down.* No, more than that, in defiance I wanted to rip the signs off and toss them over the white bridge. I felt the rage rise. I wanted the wind to carry my rage to the top of the mountain and to wash it ashore with the waves on the whites-only beaches on the other side. *This is not humane; we shouldn't have to live like this. We are citizens of this country too.*

But I didn't; of course I didn't. I just stood near the empty benches like everyone else; my brown skin and curly hair did not allow me to sit down. And when the train arrived, I waited until the doors of the non-white carriage opened before climbing in. I couldn't even bring myself to sit down. I just stood holding the rail and stared out the window.

I felt tormented about the life I was born into and grew up with. I had no role models, no one to guide me or to aspire to be like.

Every coloured person who had the ability to achieve had to leave the country to reach their potential. Talented coloured athletes could never compete against white athletes or represent South Africa. I could not see the point in people wasting their time to compete in such a limited field. They would never reach their full potential.

So many things reminded me of Dad. He had been repulsed when coloured beauty queen Pearl Jansen, our short-lived role model, had the opportunity to represent South Africa a few years prior. When pictures of Pearl were splashed all over the newspapers and news broke of her selection to compete in the Miss World pageant, she became an instant celebrity. She had reached the ultimate heights in the beauty queen stakes to jointly represent South Africa at the Miss World pageant in England in 1970. Only, she had a separate title, Miss Africa South, to that of the white young woman, Jillian Jessop, who *was* crowned Miss South Africa.

We all held our breath, waiting for the announcement of the results of the Miss World pageant, where Pearl Jansen represented every coloured young woman.

'Pearl came second,' shouted Frances as she burst through the door, clutching the newspaper with a full-length photograph of a radiant Pearl and the headline: PEARL SECOND.

In smaller print, it said Jillian Jessop, Miss South Africa, was fourth runner-up.

'She is beautiful,' said Mum holding up the front page of the newspaper. 'An ordinary factory worker from the Cape Flats, and now she is an international star.'

Dad didn't agree, as Pearl was not recognised as a representative by everyone in her own country.

He asked Mum, 'Where is this country called Africa South? Have any of you heard about that country? She should not have entered the pageant because there is no such country.'

But Mum dismissed Dad's opinion. 'This could have been our one of our daughters.'

Dad, who was clearly not able to dampen our spirits about Pearl's achievement, said, 'Over my dead body would I have allowed one of my daughters to represent a non-existent country.'

That was a momentous event in our history, and because of her win it felt that the doors were opening ever so slightly, albeit not as equal citizens. Many of us proudly displayed pictures of Pearl, adorned in her Miss Africa South sash, on our bedroom walls. For the next few years South Africa sent two entrants to the Miss World pageant until it was scrapped by the international organisation. Pearl's victory and her smiling face splashed over the newspapers had left many of us proud to be coloured.

Now, a few years later, being coloured meant that doors to employment opportunities would still slam in our faces and that owning property in areas of our own choice would continue to be prohibited by law. We had no choice but to get on with life and continue planning our future in a segregated society, and to forget about our dreams of equality in our lifetime.

Chris didn't like dancing. His great passion was the movies. When he took me on my first visit to Sunset Drive-in to see Steve McQueen in *Papillon*, I had my first opportunity to show my reckless defiance towards the segregation laws. Like most places, Sunset Drive-in had two entrances, with a fence dividing the two sections by race, and everyone looking at the same screen.

On our arrival at the non-white entrance we were disappointed when we saw the 'sold-out' sign. In a split second, with the car's headlamps turned off, Chris decided to drive to the exit lane of the whites-only section.

'Shall I, do it?' he smiled at me, tilting his head towards the lane entrance.

'No, you are going to get us thrown in jail,' I laughed nervously.

'Quick, get down on the backseat and cover yourself,' he lowered his voice, almost as if someone was listening.

In complete darkness, he slowly reversed up the lane, manoeuvring the car with great skill until he reached a spot next to a speaker. The movie had already started. He waited a few moments before rolling down the window and carefully pulled the speaker inside the car.

'I'll remain in the front seat in case we have to make a quick get-away,' he chuckled.

'I am staying here in the backseat covered under the blanket,' I said, until only my eyes showed.

That evening we watched *Papillon* in silence, with Chris constantly looking around for a torchlight whenever he heard voices nearby. During the interval, unable to go into the whites-only cafeteria to get refreshments, we remained in the car. But not even that could dampen my spirits. In a small way we had beaten the law. For the first time, I sat in the whites-only side to watch a movie. It was no different to sitting on the non-white side. We breathed the same air.

It wasn't an earth-shattering victory, but it was the defiance, albeit humiliating, that increased my resolve to not be seen as a second-class citizen. The many sacrifices Mum had made, the hardships she had endured, were real and could not be taken lightly. There was nothing I could do about the law, but there was a fire within my soul that no legislation could extinguish.

That profound moment when I realised that my simple upbringing had expired, that this was me now, my generation, and that going forward this was all that mattered. In my mind, I now challenged Mum's resolve to play it safe, to stay within our boundaries and to stick to a mapped-out life.

CAPE TOWN, SOUTH AFRICA: EARLY 1975, SUMMER

Feeling stifled at the building company, I decided to find another job where my skills would be better utilised.

Recklessly, I resigned from my job before I had secured another role. I wanted to pursue more studies to improve my career aspirations and took up a part-time role with the Drop Inn, a liquor chain, in Lansdowne while I completed another accounting course.

The Drop Inn, with its segregated shops, was owned by the Berk family. It had a few other branches around Cape Town. I was attracted to the development opportunities the manager had offered at the interview, and took up the part-time role. The retail environment was so different to my previous job, busy and customer-focussed, with many staff members in my age group.

There I met Philip, one of the sons, who had moved to the United States where he worked as a journalist. Whenever he returned to South Africa, he would work at the store. On a few occasions, Philip and I spent hours together counting hundreds of bottles of alcohol during stock audits. He was different to the other brothers, like a breath of fresh air; he had a sensitivity about him and treated the non-white staff as equals.

Many years later I nearly fell off the couch when I recognised Philip on television during the screening of the annual Golden Globes, where he was the then Head of the Hollywood Foreign Press.

I regularly followed Philip's interviews with the stars in *Filmink*, a magazine available in Australia. We were able to meet up when he was invited to attend the Sydney Film Festival one year.

The Drop Inn is also where I first met Molly, who worked in the non-white store and was much older than me. I was drawn to her straightforwardness and defiance towards authority. Funny and outspoken, she loved telling stories about growing up in Newlands before it was declared a white area. A single mother of three adult children, she was the eternal optimist whose motherly instincts embraced everyone in need of support.

Molly and I started travelling to work together and socialised on the weekends. She was popular among the black customers, and the non-white store was usually bustling with shebeen owners buying up their quotas set by the government. The shebeen owners went to great lengths to conceal their stock, some burying their supplies in holes in the ground with elaborate retrieving mechanisms in place.

Under the Liquor Act, blacks *were* allowed to purchase a limited amount of alcohol at the bottle stores but could not consume it in public places. Because bottle stores closed at midday on a Saturday, Molly, partly driven by her sales quota but more often sympathetic to their plight, illegally over-supplied black shebeen owners.

One day, during a spot raid Molly was caught by the inspectors for over-supplying black customers and she was arrested. She spent the night in jail before she was bailed out, and the case was eventually squashed. Molly became everyone's hero and we suspected that secret deals had been made to secure her release.

After that Molly was moved to the non-white store in the head office in Diep River.

'Ask them to move you to the head office,' she urged. 'This place is so much quieter and the people are really good to work with.'

'I'll have to find out if there are any positions,' I said, cottoning on to the idea of working closer to home and, of course, to be closer to Molly.

'Or tell that boyfriend of yours to put a ring on your finger, then, when you have him trapped, you can be a lady of leisure,' she chuckled.

Chris found it harder to leave at night. We spent many hours sitting in his car in front of our house; that was the only privacy we had. He wanted to be with me whenever he could.

'I am so lonely when I am away from you,' he complained regularly.

A few months later, Mum allowed me to go with Chris, along with a church group, on a bus trip to Namaqualand in South West Africa. This was the first time I went away with him. We were both excited about being able to spend the time together away from home. Our plans of spending time alone were soon thwarted: there were separate sleeping arrangements at the mission station.

I would finally be able to see the places that Mr Khune had told us about so many years ago. I was not disappointed. The trip was arranged to coincide with the spring season, a time when everything was ablaze with colour. That land and the little town that Mr Khune came from looked exactly as he had described it. Gazing across the fields of colourful daisies and the vast open spaces, I longed to visit him to let him know that I had been there. But sadly, Mr Khune had passed away a few years previously.

We spent the weekend at the old Methodist Mission Station. Inside the church was an ancient organ that had not been played since the missionaries left many years earlier. Chris sat down and played the organ, pumping the pedals furiously to keep time. Word quickly spread that someone had arrived to play the organ, and locals gathered in the church. That evening Chris played a few songs and the following morning he played at the church service.

I looked on proudly as people gathered around him and asked him to come back and play for them, or even to come and live in Namaqualand.

Two months later Chris unexpectedly proposed, on the beach. I was completely taken aback and wanted time to prepare for marriage. With both of us living at home, we knew that if we wanted to be together, then we had to get married. I thought we would wait a few years before taking that step but Chris was in a hurry for us to be together forever.

'I have had enough of tearing myself away from you at night and going home to my lonely room,' he said, wrapping his arms tightly around me.

'But you are still an apprentice and I don't know if we can afford to get married yet. We have no money, and like you, I give my salary to my mother every month.'

Traditionally, at the time, particularly in coloured families, as soon as we started earning money, our parents would manage it. We would be given pocket money, even as adults, and our income would form part of the household budget. Some were lucky enough to pay a certain amount for board and keep the rest. At home, we handed our money to Mum. When Frances and Georgie reached the age of 21, they could pay board.

'I know, but soon I will be qualified and then I can get a government subsidy to help us buy our first home,' Chris said reassuringly. 'I dream about us being together day and night. Let's not wait, I want to marry you now.'

Civil servants were granted a housing subsidy allowance. This was later extended to include coloured workers such as teachers and others who worked in civil service jobs. Chris worked for the South African Naval Dockyard which classed him as a civil servant. The subsidy, up to 40% of a mortgage repayment, gave civil servants greater opportunities to become homeowners.

'You will have to ask my mother for my hand in marriage,' I said. 'I will be the first one to get married in our family. Frances is older but she is still single and my mother might say I am too young.'

'I will ask her, just leave it to me,' he sounded so confident. 'So, Miss Crosher, will you marry me?'

'Give me a week,' I laughed. 'But for now, the answer is yes."

12

WEDDING PLANS

Mum's reaction was different to what I had expected. I knew she had given Chris her blessing but when I talked to her about our wedding plans, she referred to our wedding as sometime in the distant future. As if she wasn't ready for me to leave home yet.

Frances showed even less interest. She had recently broken up with her latest boyfriend and she was *not* enthralled with my blossoming love life. Georgie was only interested in how many bridesmaids I was planning to have, and who they would be.

'Please don't make it a family affair by asking your sisters and cousins to be bridesmaids,' Georgie laughed with that twinkle in his eye. 'Get some fresh new faces, non-family and preferably unattached. I will take good care of them.'

I was brooding over my lack of independence, engaged to be married, but still under Mum's watchful eye. The time had come for me to ask her about handling my own finances. It took a lot of courage, but it was time for me to start setting up my own home with Chris. We had plans of building our own house and he had already been looking at available plots in our surrounding area.

I found Mum doing the ironing in her bedroom, piles of ironing stood on the bed next to her. Mum, who enjoyed ironing, even pressed the dishcloths before packing them in the drawer.

'Keep the smooth edge of towels and sheets facing you,' Mum would show us. 'That way everything lines up neatly and you can open up your cupboards for anyone to inspect.'

I walked back and forth a few times past her bedroom before I mustered the courage to broach the subject. When I entered, Mum started talking about her plans for my future.

'Firstly, we must start planning for your twenty-first birthday celebration next year. I have asked Mr Jacobs to make your twenty-first key,' she said.

'I don't think that we want to wait until the end of next year, Mum,' I said softly, careful not to sound disrespectful.

'But you must have a twenty-first birthday celebration, like Frances and Georgie had,' she insisted.

'Mum, we want to get married a year from now. We would rather save that money you are planning to spend on my birthday party towards a deposit on a plot to build a house.'

I was hoping that Mum would be happy about my plan. I knew she would be impressed if she understood that we wanted to build a house.

It was then that I seized the moment.

'Mum,' I said hesitantly. 'I have been giving all my money to you every month ever since I started working. But now I would like to start managing my money so that I can prepare for my wedding next year.'

The ticking sound of the clock on the bedside table became louder as a silence hung in the air. Placing the freshly ironed shirt on a wooden clothes hanger, Mum squeezed the cloth, letting the water drip into the bowl next to her.

Straightening out my blue skirt she said, 'This is a time-consuming skirt to press, there are so many pleats.'

Neatly she smoothed out the skirt, then folded the pleats in straight lines, before spreading the wet cloth on top. Before picking up the hot iron, she dipped her hand into the bowl and sprinkled more water over the cloth. I loved my pleated skirt, it was so in fashion.

'Mum are you listening to me?' I blurted out. 'I have no money saved and I will need to buy lots of things for my wedding and for our new home. I am almost twenty years old. I can't keep giving my salary to you every month. Is it yes or no? Answer me now, please.'

Mum looked down at the ironing table. I immediately felt sorry for attacking her so bluntly and stood waiting for her response, a little unsure if this was the right moment to have approached her.

A few moments passed, then finally, without looking at me, Mum gestured with her head towards her wardrobe.

'Put your hand between my clothes on the top shelf,' she instructed. 'Between the blue and red jerseys.'

With my back turned to Mum, I slid my hand between the blue and red jerseys and found three brown envelopes. *Frances, Georgie, Beryl,* I read to myself as I flicked through them.

'Open yours.'

Inside the envelope was a stack of notes held together with an elastic band. I stood looking down at the envelope, tears streamed down my face. Behind me the hissing of the hot iron on the wet cloth filled my ears as Mum continued pressing the pleats of my blue skirt.

'I have been saving your money ever since you started working. I knew this day would come and I wanted you to be ready for it.'

I stood holding the envelopes, my face hot and sticky as the tears flowed. I wanted to throw my arms around her, but when I turned around to face her, she thrust a bunch of clothes hangers with my freshly ironed clothes into my hands.

'We'll go next Saturday to do some shopping and make a lay-by, and then go and see your aunty about your wedding dress,' she said.

The following week, with the brown envelope containing my savings tucked in my bag, Mum and I set off on our shopping trip to Wynberg, our main shopping district. Our relationship was now on a whole new level. We talked about household items, fabric for my wedding dress and what colour I would have for the bridesmaids.

All the bigger retail stores were on Main Street: Ackermans, Woolworths and the big variety store OK Bazaars. With my arm hooked into Mum's we walked in and out of the shops, happily buying linen and other household items. At Rifkin and Miller, the drapery store with their slogan *'From a Needle to an Anchor'*, Mum bought my first sewing kit.

Looking down at the sewing box with a variety of sewing needles, a metal thimble and variety of coloured cotton cones, I wondered if I'd ever use this. When Mum showed me a grater, tea strainer and dish clothes, it dawned on me that I would be having my own kitchen soon. I had seen these items in our house but never thought that one day I would be setting up my own home.

I felt ready to spend the rest of my life with Chris. There was nothing I wanted more than to be married and live in my own house with plenty of rooms and space— the closest to finally having my own bedroom.

'I never had any of these things when I got married,' Mum said. 'I didn't have anyone to help me prepare for my wedding. I gathered a few used items from the hotel where I worked, and that is how I started off. So, I have made a list of things that you will need to set up your new home.'

Around me, life was changing rapidly. In January 1976, television was introduced in South Africa. Hard-line government leaders, like the assassinated Prime Minister Hendrick Verwoerd, and the conservative Minister for Posts and Telegraphs, Dr Albert Hertzog, had ruled television as a worldly evil. Dr Hertzog feared that television would expose people to films showing interracial mixing.

Television coverage started daily at 6 pm until 11 pm, on one channel with programmes equally split between English and Afrikaans. Only white people appeared on locally-produced television programmes.

On weekends, additional time was devoted to sport. How I wished Dad could have seen these sports programmes.

As the months went by, our household was abuzz with wedding plans and details of my wedding dress, designed and made by Mum's sister, was kept secret. An afternoon tea was arranged with a few ladies in our neighbourhood to inspect my trousseau while Mum gave them details of my wedding plans.

Mum had started collecting chicken wishbones and empty egg cartons. These items were used to create wedding decorations. Wishbones were dried, sanded and sprayed gold, for good luck. Egg cartons were cut out, sprayed silver, and tied with ribbon to resemble wedding bells. Mum had every detail planned. She spent many hours making fancy candles for the tables with hot wax poured over the candles while swirling them in cold water.

In the week before our wedding the students had started boycotting classes and the unrest had spilled over into our streets. The 1st of May, the International Worker's Day, was a celebration of the roles played by the Trade Unions, the Communist Party and other labour movements against apartheid. This was also linked to the sporadic unrest where the police used teargas and rubber bullets to disperse crowds of students and protesters.

Our streets were littered with burning tyres and protesters hurled large stones at public buses, causing the police to set up roadblocks. The murmuring on the Cape Flats was that students were preparing to take up the fight against gutter education.

I woke up to a rainy wedding day. The night before Mum and I had talked about Dad. I wondered if I would have been getting married now if he was still alive. That night, I thought about the many conversations Dad and I had about life and about being the best person I could be.

'Do you think Dad will be proud of me?' I asked Mum. 'If only he was younger when you got married, then he would still have been alive today.'

'Your father lived for you children. And, you always had time for him; you were the only one who listened to him. Your father really wasted his life away, he could not cope with the hard times. I knew that one day, all of you would grow up and life would become easier.'

My godfather had arrived to accompany me into the church. My heart ached for Dad. He would have been standing next to me. My world would have felt right, complete.

That afternoon, while Mum pinned my veil, everyone prayed that the rain would ease to allow me to walk to the car. Outside the neighbours, sheltered under umbrellas, clapped and cheered when I appeared at the door. As Ismail George, our wedding car driver, made his way down Retreat Road to St Mary's Church, the streets were littered with burnt-out tyres and rocks, remnants of the recent unrest.

I was on the verge of making big changes that would shape the rest of my life. At that moment I had no fear, it felt right. I was about to marry Chris, the person who taught me how to love, how to live and how to stop beating myself up about the shortcomings in our life in the housing estate. I knew, from watching him and being with him, that my life would grow. I felt free, in love, and filled with excitement about leaving the estate.

Our wedding reception was a magical night, filled with family and friends. Father Pathe, who had become a close family friend, performed the marriage ceremony and proposed the toast at the reception. He gave a heart-warming account of his first meeting with me, as a young girl and my subsequent involvement with the youth club and other parish activities. I felt tears welling in my eyes when he remembered Dad during his speech.

'When times are tough and the challenges in your marriage arise, focus on each other, keep thinking about things that will make *each other* happy,' he said. 'Make that your thought every morning and focus less on what will make *you* happy.'

Our wedding night was nothing the way I had imagined it would be. We returned to Mum's house to get a few hours of sleep and for me to wash the lacquer out of my hair. I eventually fell asleep, exhausted, in my single bed while Chris slept on the other bed across from mine.

Our honeymoon, a drive to George and Knysna on the Garden Route, had to be delayed until the Sunday afternoon because of petrol restrictions. Garages closed on Friday afternoons and reopened Monday mornings. This meant that we had to fill containers with petrol in readiness for our departure, and one container to keep in the boot of the car.

When it was time to leave, Mum cried and held on to me as if she would never see me again. As usual Georgie offered us some marital advice, in his jovial manner. Frances tried to hide her sadness by joking about my going-away outfit, a cream knitted top, brown skirt and brown boots. Maureen and Andy stood waving as we drove down the street.

Very soon we would move into our new home. Just the two of us. That was progress. No longer would I be a part of the housing estate, where I felt like a downtrodden person. Our new house, away from the housing estate, a free-standing house on our piece of land, was about to be built. We had picked out the colours, the polished floors, two bathrooms and enough bedrooms for our future children.

This was what Mum had sacrificed her life for and constantly pushed us to do—to keep moving forward.

Her words over the years now had meaning, 'Don't think about apartheid and how the government is ruling your life. You must create your own life. If I let apartheid distract me while you were growing up, then you would have been washing dishes in the bakery and serving on white people.'

These very words of wisdom lifted my soul and sent it soaring. I looked at her standing at the gate waving. It was as if I now saw her through different eyes. Mum's eyes, still moist with tears, sparkled in the light, her smile lit up her face. She was still waving when we turned the corner at the end of our street.

Even the darkness which so often engulfed my vision whenever I looked at the house and street was lifted.

Driving over Sir Lowry's Pass, along the Garden Route, we passed the white-owned apple farms at Elgin and Grabouw and headed towards Swellendam and Mossel Bay. These country towns, where Afrikaners owned most of the land, had a reputation for poor treatment of non-white farm workers. And that was evident by the dismissive way in which they treated us in the shops we stopped at.

One of the highlights for me was seeing the spectacular Hottentots Holland mountain range, with clouds covering its peaks. These were the things that white people could not own; it belonged to all of us.

'One arm around my wife, the other on the wheel,' Chris sang to his own tune as we drove along the endless Garden Route.

'*Your* wife? Don't think you own me,' I laughed. 'I am my father's child and that mysterious St Helena blood runs through my veins. I may be a descendant of a slave, but don't think of me as *your* slave.'

His wife! I pondered on that thought. This was not just a honeymoon; this meant that I could not go home to my bedroom. It would be just the two of us, every day and every night. Chris seemed so comfortable, so happy with me by his side, as if his life was complete. The thought of spending the rest of my life with him seemed natural. A way out of our crowded home and the restrictions placed on me. Still, fears kept creeping into my mind. *Is this what I really want to do with the rest of my life?*

As we sped along the open road, mesmerised by the beauty, I marvelled at the vastness of our province. With the windows tightly shut to keep out the cold wind, we chatted about our wedding and the many gifts still unopened. Unable to sit down in the few cafés along the way, we ate our meals in the car.

Toilets and beaches, libraries and museums entrances, all clearly marked 'European Only'.

It was dark when we eventually reached Sedgefield, a small coastal town between George and Knysna. The owners, who were Afrikaners, took us to a small room around the back. I was too exhausted to care about our surroundings, and the small room was a welcome respite from the long drive. The place had been recommended by one of Chris's relatives who lived in George. In the darkness it didn't look impressive, but we were pleasantly surprised by our surroundings in the morning.

The small Bed & Breakfast was set in luscious beauty and the lagoon added to the tranquility of the surroundings. Our breakfast was served in a smaller area while the rest of the white guests ate in a separate area.

'I wonder why they allowed you to book in here,' I said to Chris on the second morning. 'This looks like a place for whites only.'

'I am sure they realise that they need the money and that is why they take bookings from non-whites in the off-season,' he said. 'Either way, we are not staying in this *verkrampte* place to be treated like we are their servants,' he added, using the Afrikaans word for reactionary racists.

Shaking his head, he said, 'You do know that we are sleeping in the servants' quarters, don't you? But while you were sleeping, I called my cousins in East London, and they are expecting us tomorrow.'

Another adventure awaited as we set off on the long road. Chris's relatives welcomed us with open arms. Mr Segers' brother, Sonny Segers, was an active member of the Coloured Persons Representative Council (CPRC). This council was established to represent coloured people in government, but it had lacked the power to change or influence legislation.

When Uncle Sonny talked politics, I was immediately reminded of how Dad used to trivialise the relevance of the CPRC. I remembered how Dad used to talk of the CPRC: 'Just a whole lot of fools dancing to the tune of the government. Instead of demanding *equal* rights, they are agreeing to maintain *separate* rights. They should sack the lot of them.'

Uncle Sonny too seemed disillusioned with the CPRC and blamed the in-fighting and power struggles within the council for its failures.

I learnt from Uncle Sonny that, as the government did with black people, some of those in power had plans to establish a coloured homeland. The CPRC, he said, had fought against those plans, and eventually this initiative was abandoned.

After a fun-filled three weeks exploring the Eastern Cape, it was time to return home and back to our jobs. Young, in love and carefree, we had spent every last cent. Chris made no secret of how much he adored me. Street-wise and confident, he knew how to make our last bit of petrol last until we reached home. As we sped along the majestic highways back over Sir Lowry's Pass, he'd switch off the car and let it roll downhill for as far as he could.

For me, a girl from the Cape Flats, this wild adventure, was something that I had never imagined would happen to me.

We stayed with Chris's parents while we waited for work to commence on our new home. Mrs Segers, as I continued to address her, had never fully accepted that her son had married a girl from the council housing estate. She made no secret of her displeasure at having me as part of the family, most times excluding me as a member of the household.

We remained civil towards one another but never engaged in casual conversation, unless we were forced to. Both of us tried, on various occasions, but the framed picture of his previous girlfriend on her bedside table had cemented our rift.

Mr Segers, who was always on the defensive about his wife's behaviour, tried his best to make me feel welcome in their home.

At times, I longed for our small home in the housing estate, to listen to Mum's wisdom and to join in the laughter and fun.

13

POLITICAL CHAOS

A month after our wedding, the political landscape in the country shifted. In the black township of Soweto in Johannesburg, during the month of June 1976, students protested against a government directive which made Afrikaans the compulsory medium of instruction in local schools. The call for peaceful protests spread rapidly to other provinces, and in the Western Cape coloured high schools heeded the call.

Police often resorted to using teargas and batons to take back control of the streets and to send a clear message to protesters. Peaceful protest marches and rallies turned into battlefields, with police using extreme violence against unarmed students.

As the student boycotts intensified over the weeks and months, our streets were filled with burning tyres and rocks used to stone public buses and cars. Police armoured vehicles, known as casspirs, were ever-present in our areas. These were protests unlike any we had ever seen.

Defiant masses of coloured university and high school students carrying placards demanding 'Down with gutter education' and black students carrying ones saying 'Down with Bantu Education' were confronted daily by armed police. For the first time, white students at the University of Cape Town supported the call and held peaceful marches, giving the black power salute.

The authorities reacted by imposing bans on public gatherings, but defiant students continued their protests. These protests were met with the full force of the law. When teargas and batons failed to bring about results, police retaliated with live ammunition.

In our suburb, rampaging students were met with armed police in our main street. A young man known to us was shot dead by police during one of the clashes. That sent shockwaves through our community, with parents forbidding their children from participating in the uprising. Maureen and Andy were at high school and their safety was Mum's main concern. They were forbidden from participating in any marches and kept home during the extreme unrest.

Every so often, I thought of Dad's predictions so many years ago that the government won't be in power forever. He could not have predicted that a student uprising would cause the shift in the political landscape. He had hopes that the demise of power would come from within the ruling National Party.

A few months later, I was surprised to receive a promotional transfer to the Drop Inn head office in Diep River. It meant a pay rise and working closer to home. Elated about seeing Molly again, we planned on travelling together. I had passed my driving test before our wedding, and now I started driving the car to work every day.

In the head office, I was the youngest and *only* coloured person in the administration office, with six white staff members. During morning tea they gathered in a group around the coffee table. On the first day, when I continued working while they stopped for coffee, they informed me that morning tea and lunch was available for me in the coloured shop downstairs.

The director, an Afrikaner, was always openly dismissive of me and excluded me from any conversations, other than work instructions. He talked and joked with the other staff members but ignored me completely. The atmosphere was stifled and my feelings of optimism about a future career in this organisation soon disappeared. I longed for the camaraderie of the Lansdowne branch, the small back office, and the relaxed and inclusive atmosphere.

In the western Cape, as the months progressed, the political landscape worsened. The student uprising that had started in Soweto, continued to spread rapidly through our city.

The students, relentless in their stance against the authorities, boycotted classes and general unrest ensued with public buses and cars stoned. The words on everyone's lips were that the revolution had begun. Placard-bearing students gathered at rallies, displaying their strong messages of frustration and rage against inequality.

Police brutality towards students only reinforced their resolve to continue the fight. The uprising, which had begun in Soweto in 1976, had swept the nation, waiting to ignite and explode again. Over the months, many young people had lost their lives in the struggle for freedom.

Young people who were caught up in the euphoria of defying the authorities showed a resolved that their parents never did. They were on the path to freedom, and the realisation had set in that the fight for equality would be a hard-fought battle—one they had to be prepared to die for. The police went into battle, showing no restraint. They were not only there to uphold the law but mostly to defend *their* land, even if it meant shooting to kill.

One evening, I received a phone call from Frances to come home. She said that she had exciting news to share.

'Mum, I am getting married,' she said smiling broadly.

I looked over at Mum, who sat staring at Frances for a few moments. Holding my breath, I waited for Mum's reaction. Slowly she picked up her cup of tea, and then smiled. I could exhale.

'When are you planning to get married?' I asked, still not able to grasp the news.

My question ignored, I sensed that there was more to this announcement. Then came the bombshell. Mum moved around nervously in her chair as Frances uttered the words that she least expected.

'I am pregnant,' she beamed, as if it was the most natural thing in the world.

Once the shock of this news sunk in, Mum immediately sprang into action to plan the wedding. Looking at the calendar, Frances announced that she wanted to get married in December. Mum began rattling off everything that needed to happen for her wedding. This was a new era in our family: the next generation was about to enter this life. Mum's first grandchild.

I had not given a thought to starting a family until I watched Frances's growing belly. Chris and I had, up to that point, enjoyed a care-free married life. Our new-found freedom allowed us to go out partying till all hours and go to the movies up to three times a week. But now the thought of a baby was intriguing.

After their wedding, Frances and her husband moved in to live with Mum. Both Mum and I started buying baby clothes, and the excitement was mounting for this momentous occasion. Frances suffered severe bouts of morning sickness throughout her pregnancy, and Mum tried hard to coax her into eating. Chris and I visited Mum's house more frequently, and Frances and I grew closer than we had ever been. We now had a common bond, married life.

Georgie was still enjoying his life with a new woman on his arm every week. He looked far from settling down and moved in and out of Mum's house as it suited him. Every woman he met was introduced to Mum as her future daughter-in-law. With Maureen and Andy now well into their teens, Mum now had more time to herself since Dad's death, three years earlier.

What happened during the 1976 student uprising had changed the South African political landscape forever. Over the months the students' rage against the authorities intensified, and driven by the senseless deaths of many young people the riots continued.

During 1977, pressure from the international community against the apartheid government grew. Calls for international sporting boycotts were stepped up and overseas trade sanctions increased. Activism reached new heights; because of the Illegal Gathering Act, public rallies were not openly held. Anti-apartheid leaders, pursued relentlessly by the authorities, were detained without trial. Many fled to neighbouring countries or overseas, banned from living in their own country.

Two days before the anniversary of the June 1976 student uprising, Frances gave birth to Mum's first grandson, David. His arrival was a distraction from what was happening on our streets. Mum and I prepared the room for their homecoming. David, a chubby-cheeked baby, was handed from arm to arm as we came to terms with Frances being a mother and our family now into its next generation.

Over the strike period, the *Cape Herald*, the only newspaper staffed by coloured journalists, reported on the riots and the mood of the people. Many coloured journalists were activists and able to get information not available to white journalists. The investigations and subsequent revelations in the press had the authorities hounding them for their sources. Some journalists were detained and others fled the country.

The uprising had sent a clear message to the authorities that the oppressed had reached a stage of revolt.

The unions and student movement called on workers to join a two-day strike on the anniversary of the June 1976 student uprising. Both Chris and I were eager to support the strike, hoping that we could be part of the growing opposition to the government's divisive policies. On Thursday and Friday, 16-17 June 1977, along with many workers, we supported the call.

Shortly after arriving at work the next Monday I was summoned to the manager's office. In the presence of the accountant, I was interrogated about my participation in the strike and advised of the Workers Act on strike action.

Under this Act, I was advised, the company had the right to deduct four days' pay.

Trying to hide my anger and the rising heat in my cheeks, I lowered my eyes. *Don't cry*, I willed myself. But I could not stop the tears forming in my eyes. My fingers tightened as I clenched my fists.

'What do you, as a coloured person, think this strike will achieve?' the manager asked, his lips curling into a half smile. 'You do realise that nothing will come of this action. Next week all this will be forgotten, and like us, you will have to carry on working.'

'How can you deduct *four* days?' I stammered, staring him in the face this time, and then said defiantly, 'I don't work weekends.'

Rising from his chair, the manager walked closer to me until he was within arm's length of my face, and said, 'Because the Act says so. Go and ask your union leaders, if you don't believe me.'

The accountant, who had not said a word, shifted his body weight from one leg to the other. Quietly I walked back to my desk, the eyes of the rest of the white staff lowered as they carried on working.

I wanted to believe that the other staff were not gloating. I needed their support but instead a silence hung over the office, the sound of calculators and shuffling papers audible. Through my tears, I reached for the pile of invoices on my desk and started working.

During the morning tea break, I rushed downstairs to the coloured shop where Molly worked. The sight of her smiling face unleashed my pent-up emotions. Through my sobs, I recounted the humiliating experience.

'I am not going back up there, I am resigning,' I sobbed as she tried to make light of the situation by imitating her manager who had told her the same thing.

'You will do no such thing,' she said sternly. 'Don't you dare weaken. In fact, wait, I have a solution. Believe me, this will make you smile from deep inside of you every time you think of me.'

Casually she walked over to the crates containing three-gallon glass cans. Smiling as if she was checking the shelf in front of her, she cracked the seals of the cans.

'Close your mouth,' she said. 'There, are you happy now, that'll compensate for some of our loss of wages. Now run upstairs like a good girl and get back to work, I'll see you at lunch time.'

Thanks to Molly's actions, I couldn't stop smiling. Back at my desk I continued working in silence. I tried hard to find my place in that office but it became unbearable. I also knew that chances of a promotion under this manager were impossible.

It was the most difficult period of my working life. I was desperately unhappy at work and could not settle. It was pure torture coming into the office every day, feeling like an outsider. I resigned at the end of that month.

Little did I know that I was pregnant. With everything going on around us, that was the furthest thought from my mind. Chris and I were both thrown by the news that parenthood was upon us. My immediate concern was trying to find work while pregnant.

'What about our new house?' I asked, my tears not far away.

'We'll manage,' Chris said reassuringly. 'I am sure you are entitled to some unemployment benefits as well. Don't despair, it's not good for you or the baby.'

Mum, still recovering from her first grandchild, was bursting with excitement at the news. Our family was growing rapidly and Mum was satisfied that she had set us all on the right path to build our futures.

When Chris shared the news with his parents, they were both delighted. Mr Segers started making plans immediately to make a cot and other baby furniture. Mrs Segers, with whom my rift had widened, tried her best to contribute. But I was hurt and struggled with her indifference towards me. That photograph was still next to her bed.

After an uneventful pregnancy, Sasha, a healthy little girl with tufts of black hair, was born on 25 January 1978. Her placid demeanour made motherhood a joy. I was nearly 23 years old and now a mother. Yet while our lives had economically improved, we were far from living in a free society. Frances and I had now birthed two children into this segregated society. Our children had small grey identity books with the 01 number at the end. This automatically determined their future; they would be classified as Cape Coloureds and live as second-class citizens.

'We can't let our children grow up in this society,' Frances would say whenever we discussed the state of the nation. 'This is an abnormal society. We owe it to our children to give them the freedom they deserve.'

It was then that Frances started talking about moving her family to Australia. Friends of hers had made the move a few months prior. Mum encouraged them to go and for all of us to think about leaving the country.

But for us, the focus was elsewhere. After many delays, amid all the protests and upheaval, we were finally able to move into our new home. While our streets were burning, we began our life in the refuge of our own home. Mum helped with decorating and unpacking the many boxes of trousseau that we bought on our shopping spree a few years before.

The thought of us leaving the country was not a priority. For Frances, it was different. She was determined that David would grow up in a free society. Mum raised the subject with us from time to time, but with a new mortgage it seemed impossible.

When Sasha was a month old, Maureen, who had just finished high school, was pregnant by her young apprentice boyfriend. Mum was devastated. The young man, who was raised by a single mother, came from a prominent fishing family. His mother was adamant that they should get married and for Maureen not to be an unwed mother. She also expressed her wish not to have her first grandchild born out of wedlock.

Maureen, young and confused, was encouraged to get married. Mum agreed and four months later they married. She moved in with her mother-in-law and became part of their family. We seldom saw Maureen until she gave birth later that year to Mum's third grandchild, Tracey-Lee. Maureen had been absorbed by her new family, but the birth of her daughter slowly brought my sister back to us.

Maureen had changed. After the birth of her baby

she was desperately unhappy in her marriage. Her youth was the major factor. She quietly suffered at the hands of her possessive husband. Her mother-in-law desperately wanted the marriage to work and tried her best to keep them together. But, with their youth and inability to cope with the responsibilities thrust on them, the marriage was doomed.

Andy was still in high school and lived with Mum. Georgie drifted in and out of Mum's house, from one relationship to another. He was always attracted to women much older than him. He lived the party life, drinking and spending his money on women. He drove from Cape Town to Johannesburg for work or wherever he met a woman. I was alarmed at his excessive drinking habits. But he brushed it aside as nothing to be concerned about.

When Sasha was a year old, I joined Frances working part-time for a prominent Indian family. The Patels owned several businesses, including the popular coloured cinemas, the Kismet and Cine 400. They were the leaders in coloured entertainment venues and we were thrilled to be on the VIP guest list when they opened the impressive Galaxy and Space Odyssey nightclubs. These iconic venues raised the bar in entertainment for coloureds.

At the Space Odyssey, in Woodstock, I saw a young pop singer, Brenda Fassie, who would become South Africa's kwaito queen. That night she performed as part of a trio called Joy. The words of their signature song, *Paradise Road*, were so fitting for Frances' farewell. It was one of South Africa's biggest hits of 1980.

In 1980 Frances and her family set off on a flight to Australia. It was an exciting time for them but a sad day for our family. This was the beginning of our family separation. Frances and I, through the birth of our children, had grown closer, like we were as teenagers. At one point, when she was frustrated with her life and with her struggle to meet a boyfriend, we had started to drift apart. But when she had found happiness, we reconnected and developed a strong bond. She was now setting off to a far-away place overseas.

When we held each other at the airport, she whispered, 'Start working on Chris and perhaps before you have another baby you can come and live with us in Australia.'

I knew that going overseas was not in our immediate future.

14

FLIGHT TO FREEDOM

South Africa: August 1980, Late Winter

Soon after their arrival in Australia, Frances's weekly letters and photographs started arriving. They described their new life in great detail: the surf at Bondi Beach; their visits to Sydney Opera House, drives over the Harbour Bridge, and their adventures on the Sydney Ferries. She compared the place where they lived to the white areas in South Africa and described how people lived freely in the area of their choice.

Some letters would be in the form of an aerogram or a postcard, but mostly it would be long letters accompanied by photographs. I would wait in anticipation for her letters to arrive, eagerly reading every morsel of their everyday life. Her letters were also filled with a great longing for us, and at the end of each letter she would remind us all to write back, as if she had not seen us for many years.

Her letters stirred a longing in me to see the places she described. The thought of discovering new places and having the freedom to live anywhere was intriguing, and it filled me with a restlessness. *Perhaps, we, should all move to Australia,* I often thought.

When I shared my feelings with Mum, she was excited about the possibility that we could all follow Frances and her family.

'It does sound like a great place to live, doesn't it, Mum?' I said during one of our discussions after we read Frances's latest letter. 'Just look at her sunning herself on a ferry. I know we've just bought a new house, but perhaps we can think about it and just make inquiries from the Australian Embassy,' I said.

'I know that if you go, then Maureen and Andy will also want to follow. I am not sure about Georgie, but who knows, he may decide as well,' said Mum.

'I think we should go into the Australian Embassy and get the information so that I can present it to Chris, and hopefully he will agree.'

I promised Mum that I would visit the Australian Embassy when I had a day off work. This thought excited me and I could not wait to share this news in my next letter to Frances. I longed to see her and for us to be close again. She had taken me under her wing from a young age and I knew that she would be bursting with curiosity as to our progress.

After Frances and I were married and had children, we had become inseparable and spent every weekend together. Before Frances and her family left for Australia they had bought a house in Mitchells Plain, a newly developed suburb for coloureds on the Cape Flats, about 32 kilometres from town.

This suburb was created to alleviate the housing shortages for coloureds who were forcibly moved out of areas now declared white. The houses were built in a standard box-like design and laid out in neat rows, with the area surrounded by bushes and sand. With limited services in place, transport was a big drawback. There were no train stations, so buses, taxis or cars were the only means of transport.

I missed Frances terribly after she left and thoughts of wanting to join her in Australia were niggling at me. During her first phone call, on a Sunday morning, from a call box in Bondi, we screamed and talked and screamed and talked until her money ran out. She wrote so positively about Australia and how they were settling in that my urge to join her grew even more as time went by.

Chris was not keen when I first broached the subject. He had started building a patio and was busy erecting a fence around our new home.

'We've only just moved in and we won't make any money on this house if we were to sell it,' he said. 'And besides, I thought that you were happy now that we have moved into our own home.'

'I just think it will be a great adventure, something different. We are still young and can start over again. I know this house is what I wanted, but I think there is so much more out there for us to experience. Just promise me that you will think about it and be open to exploring the idea.'

I knew that I had some serious convincing to do if I wanted Chris to emigrate. He was comfortable in his job, happy in our new home, and with his aging parents being able to enjoy seeing Sasha grow up, he had little intention of making drastic changes to our life. He was happy to work hard and make extra money to provide us with a good life. But every time I received a letter from Frances, I started fantasising about moving to Australia.

I then decided to gather the information and to wait for an opportunity to present it.

Meanwhile I had seen information in our church newsletter about Marriage Encounter. This was a weekend for Catholic couples to rediscover and enrich their marriages.

When I found out that this weekend coincided with our fifth wedding anniversary, I thought it would be the perfect getaway. It would also present an opportunity to openly discuss our future in a nurturing environment and this would allow me to present my case.

'There is nothing wrong with our marriage. Why do we have to go on a Marriage Encounter weekend?' Chris asked.

'It'll be an opportunity to get away for a weekend. We hardly get time away, with you working such long hours and me having to juggle work and taking care of Sasha. And besides, it is through the church and we get to stay at Maryland, a convent in Hanover Park.'

Stunned, he looked at me and said, 'Hanover Park, are you serious? In that God-forsaken place. In that concrete jungle filled with blocks of flats. What can the nuns teach us about our marriage? They've never been married!'

'This weekend is not run by the nuns. We will stay in the convent for the weekend and they provide the meals, but the weekend is run by a priest and two couples. Just come along with an open mind—and besides, I've completed the forms and sent them off. If you don't like it by Saturday afternoon, then we can leave,' I said.

Hanover Park, set in the heart of the Cape Flats, was one of the areas many coloured people were moved to and had become overcrowded with families living in large three-storey blocks of flats. From our room in the convent we could see washing lines strung between the buildings and children playing in the big courtyard.

I had no idea, at the time, that we would have to share so deeply about ourselves and that the whole weekend would consist of presentations and reflection. Even more so that the weekend was completely multiracial. I sensed Chris's tension when we arrived at the convent, especially when he was asked to remove his watch. The group leader assured him that he would get it back on Sunday night.

The first evening seemed quite strained, with everyone listening intently to the presentations. The leaders shared deeply about their marriages and I identified with so many of the issues they raised. When one of the couples shared about the pressures and distractions of daily living, my mind drifted to when we first got married.

I loved playing house, cooking, cleaning and taking care of all Chris's needs. He came from a home where his mother did everything and I was conscious to fulfil my role as his wife. Even though I came from a home where Mum was too busy working to be a housewife, I wanted to take charge of my home and create a different life. Lovingly I picked up after him, put down the toilet seat and placed the cap back on the toothpaste. This, I thought, was expected of me as his wife.

But it didn't take me long to get irritated with putting the cap back on the toothpaste or doing the dishes after dinner. I soon started making demands, telling Chris to take turns in doing the dishes, just like we had to do at home. Picking up his towels and clothes... I lovingly did that when we were newly married, but soon I realised that this was not my job. And so, early on, I set the boundaries, and Chris had no choice but to do his share if he wanted me to be happy.

Most of our disagreements were about the long hours Chris worked. He was always trying to earn extra money and was on-call to fix electrical problems, so often he left me and Sasha alone. This was one of the issues I wanted us to work on during the weekend.

Each session started with a presentation by a couple who shared deeply about their marriage and a priest who likened his relationship to God.

'I am not sharing private details of our life with strangers,' Chris whispered during one of the presentations where the couple broke down while telling their story.

'You don't have to share with anyone else, we all have the same issues anyway,' I said. 'Please keep an open mind.'

'But this is the time I could be watching Bonanza on a Friday night,' he said, rolling his eyes.

It wasn't until we were sent to separate locations to write a letter to each other that Chris started taking it seriously. This was his first letter to me since we got married, and after reading how deeply he felt about me and our life together, I knew that we did the right thing to come on this weekend.

As the weekend progressed, my letters to him were

candid. I was unhappy about continuing to live in South Africa and was opposed to subjecting our child to these laws. I felt that we should give ourselves and Sasha every opportunity to explore a life in a country where we could be free. While my letters were filled with ideas of wild adventure, his letters were measured and sensible, deeply professing his love for me.

'What works for them may not necessarily work for us,' Chris said when we finally got together to share our last topic of the evening. 'This weekend has been emotionally draining, and please don't think that I don't want to explore us moving abroad. But we have to be practical and look at what we will be sacrificing before leaping into the unknown.'

'We do have Frances and her family there. Just think about them and how they ventured there without knowing anyone in a strange country, and they are making it work,' I said.

After the final presentation on the Sunday, the leaders approached us and asked for us to remain in our rooms before the farewell Mass.

'We have been observing you during the weekend and we would like you to join our team,' one of the presenters said. 'This will involve you having to attend another weekend, and you will be assigned to a leadership couple to help you to prepare your presentations.'

Chris was clearly humbled by this gesture and held me close as we stood for a while after they left. Our book of love letters lay on the bed with the logo of two hearts intertwined on the cover. This was our fifth wedding anniversary weekend and we were faced with a major decision that would change our lives. I was ready to jump ship, but Chris was clearly torn.

That evening, the farewell Holy Mass was a moving, spiritual celebration to end a weekend of soul searching and reflection. We hugged other couples who were now no longer strangers, and shed tears as we embraced irrespective of race. Within the confines of the convent and through deep personal sharing, it seemed that thoughts of apartheid were non-existent. In this religious building, no one was better than the other.

While we were in a hurry to get back home to Sasha, this place surrounded by blocks of flats was a reminder of what the reality is. As we all drove off to our different areas, our segregated lives continued.

'This is what I am tired of. Inside that building we hugged and embraced but outside things are still the same,' I said. 'We can either be happy to live this way or we can take the chance and see what freedom will be like.'

'Let's set ourselves a time-frame,' Chris said. 'I am a great believer in destiny—if it's meant to be, then it will happen.'

'You know that I don't believe in destiny, we've got to make it happen for it to become our destiny,' I said, winking as I smiled.

I felt that the weekend was a success in that we were able to discuss calmly. We had the opportunity to share and talk through our fears should we decide to emigrate. We had agreed to explore the idea with no immediate rush.

A few weeks later I received a phone call from a couple in our parish who were also selected to go on the Marriage Encounter deeper weekend.

'My name is Patricia, I believe you have been invited to join our group. Would you be able to give us a lift to the group meeting?'

While we were in the same parish, I had never met Patricia. But on that drive to the group meeting, we struck up a firm friendship with her and her husband Charles.

Our group leaders, Sheila and Ian, a white couple who lived in Rondebosch, hosted the evening. There were four couples from different race groups; one couple from the black township of Gugulethu, and a couple from what was known as a grey area, Observatory. A grey area was a suburb close to the city where mostly reclassified people lived, not white nor black but *grey*. We were assigned to work with this couple who we assumed to be coloured.

At our first meeting we were astounded when the wife told us that she had been reclassified as white. This was the first time that I had met someone who had been reclassified.

Stunned, I listened as she explained the process. Assessed by government officials, as was everyone who wished to be reclassified, she was subjected to their grading. Her hair had to be a certain texture to allow a pencil to slide through it. If the pencil slid through, then she received an approving tick; if the pencil got stuck because her hair was curly, she failed. Her skin had to be the correct shade. Many coloured people who were able to pass these tests avoided the hot summer sun for fear of their skins turning brown. Some of the older ladies plastered their faces with powder to appear white, which would allow them the same privileges.

I could not believe that this woman had to make a

decision as immense as that.

'This is why I hate this country,' I said to Chris afterwards. 'How degrading to be subjected to such a test. I hate this government with a passion.'

'But why would you sell your soul,' Chris said. 'She has to live with giving up her family for love.'

'She was forced to. It was either that or leave the country,' I said. 'Either way she would have lost out.'

Whenever we had group meetings at Sheila and Ian's home, they were warm and friendly hosts. Hugs and warmth flowed freely and we were made to feel very comfortable inside the confines of their home. They offered a supportive environment for us to write our presentations.

One day, Chris and I walked in town when we saw Ian in the company of some work colleagues, all dressed in suits. Chris looked across at Ian to greet him, but as Ian passed he barely acknowledged us and turned his head the other way to continue talking to his colleagues.

'I am not going back to their home again,' was Chris's first comment as we walked to our car.

'I agree, I can't stand these false people. They profess to be ready and willing to embrace us—but it is on their terms,' I said. 'This is why I want to leave this place. Things won't ever change.'

Now I felt that I was slowly making headway with getting Chris to be more serious about emigration. Sasha would soon have to start school and I wanted her to do that in Australia. Frances called often to check on progress and to give us more information about what we could expect if we decided to emigrate.

When we finally submitted our application to the

Australian Embassy, I was so excited that I wanted to start packing straight away.

'They said the process could take up to a year,' Chris reminded me.

'But we don't want to be caught off-guard,' I said. 'We have to put our house on the market as well and sell our car.'

Mum was excitedly planning her first trip as well to coincide with our departure. Maureen, who had grown closer to us as Tracey grew older, also decided that she would follow with her family once we were settled. She knew that for her to join us in Australia, she would have to stay in the marriage and try to make it work. If not, then it would be against the law to leave with Tracey. Andy who was working as an apprentice panel-beater was still undecided about leaving. Georgie, who was living the single life, had no plans but promised to visit us.

But life had other plans for us. The week when we received the letter that our Australian permanent resident visas had been approved, I discovered that I was pregnant. Chris, who had taken all his accumulated leave to prepare the house for sale, was ecstatic. I was stunned and felt apprehensive about the timing. *Was this a sign? Should we wait until the baby is born and then go?* These thoughts ran through my mind.

The sale of our house went through without a hitch. And, after a spate of farewell parties, we were ready to leave.

On Friday 23 July 1982, we said our goodbyes to family and friends at DF Malan airport in Cape Town for the two-hour flight to Jan Smuts airport in Johannesburg. I was four months pregnant.

Saying goodbye to Mum was not so hard because I knew that I would see her in a couple of months for her holiday. Maureen had already applied to emigrate and they were going through the process. Georgie promised to visit soon and Andy, while still undecided, was thinking about applying as well.

Chris had a sad farewell with his parents. Mrs Segers, who was mostly bedridden after a stroke, held on to Chris as she said goodbye. It was heartbreaking to listen to her sobs as she struggled to wish him well. Mr Segers held back his tears when he greeted us, and encouraged us to go and make a better life for ourselves abroad. His tears flowed when he had to say goodbye to Sasha.

Chris's birth mother and her family came to the airport and she stood a little distance away. Her husband, with whom Chris had grown close, expressed more emotion than she did.

I was relieved when it was finally time for us to board our flight. It was my first time on a plane, and I was filled with so much excitement about the adventure that lay ahead. Chris, who had flown before from Cape Town to Durban on a family vacation, was silent during the two-hour flight. He sat in the window seat and stared at the landscape below.

Before we could board our international flight in Johannesburg, we were taken into little cubicles to be searched. Chris was searched separately from us and Sasha and I had to spread our legs while the customs officers ran their hands up and down our legs and arms. Sasha clung to me while the officers ran their hands up and down her little legs and under her arms. After scrutinising our passports, visas and luggage, we were finally on our way.

Sydney, Australia: July 1982, Late Winter

Exhausted and bleary-eyed, we arrived at Sydney Kingsford Smith airport on a rainy morning. As we walked through the exit doors I spotted Frances who was jumping up and down and waving wildly. We shed tears of joy as we embraced and hugged each other.

'Finally, you are here,' she said. 'We've been counting the hours for you to get here.'

'No more need for long letters and phone calls,' I said, hugging her and looking down at David who had grown so much in the two years since I saw him.

I felt safe in the knowledge that she was there to welcome us. The whole travel experience had been fascinating, and despite my tiredness, I tried to take in everything on the journey.

On our way to their house, while Chris and Frances chatted, I stared at our surroundings. The weather was overcast and rainy, making everything appear dark and dreary. Driving along Botany Road into Gardener's Road and then through the suburb of Earlwood, south-west of Sydney, I noticed the many dark face-brick houses, and the dilapidated buildings along the way. It looked like some of the older areas in Cape Town.

I don't know if it was tiredness or the gloomy weather, but at that very moment, I started comparing the areas in Cape Town. In the more affluent coloured areas, where people owned their homes, they were neatly rendered and painted all different colours.

The fluttering movements of the baby in my belly startled me. Placing my hand on my belly, as if to reassure the baby that everything would be fine, I felt the first pangs of homesickness.

Frances chatted non-stop, filling us in on what they had been doing and asking about everyone at home. I felt myself thinking about home, wondering what Mum was doing, and how the new owners were settling into our home. I felt a sudden longing for what was familiar to me, our home and its comforts. The realisation that now we were homeless hit me, and thoughts of starting up in a new country was suddenly daunting.

These places now looked nothing like the pictures Frances had sent. I wanted to see the beautiful beaches, landscapes and landmarks like the Sydney Opera House and the ferries on the harbour. That is what enticed me to come here. Not these dark and gloomy streets lined with lifeless face-brick houses. At that moment I decided that this place was ugly and where we came from, every-thing was better. The reasons why we had left South Africa did not enter my mind.

I disliked this place.

When we arrived at their sparsely furnished, rented semi-detached house in Campsie, I looked around and longed for my spacious house. When Frances took us to our bedroom, it was empty. She explained that they would take us to the shop to buy a mattress. I panicked: four months pregnant and tired, I needed somewhere to rest. All we had was our Travellers Cheques, but luckily the shop accepted them and Chris was able to purchase a mattress and pillows.

We had sent some household goods in a container, and fortunately the boxes had arrived, so I had some linen to make our bed on the mattress. The next day we bought a television and set it up in our bedroom, where we would spend most of our time laying down and talking about our future. Chris, who tried to be as positive as he could, assured me that as soon as he found a job, we would move into our own place.

'This is not what I expected,' I said. 'They didn't even have a bed for us to sleep on.'

As the days passed, I became increasingly negative and judgmental of how little progress Frances and her family appeared to have made.

'We might have lived in an abnormal society, but we had certain standards,' I said. 'Mum will be horrified that we have to sleep on a mattress. They must get a bed for Mum to sleep on before she arrives.'

'I know, but you must give the place a chance,' Chris said. 'Think of the reasons why we left; don't ever forget that.'

'We lived in segregated areas but we were still able to own a home. After two years here in this country, they have nothing,' I said.

'You are forgetting how difficult it must have been for them to look for work, and to set up a home, in a new country without family support,' Chris said.

In my mind, all I knew was that now, 18 months after we had decided to emigrate we had uprooted ourselves, sold our house, our car and left our secure jobs to seek freedom for our children.

Now, we had nothing.

Because of the exchange rate, we had lost half our money and we were limited to the amount of money we could take out of the country. At the time, this was set at ZAR4,000 per adult at the normal exchange rate (at the time it was about AUS$1,50 to ZAR1,00), and any funds in excess of that limit was exchanged at the 'financial rand', which was valued at a punitive twenty Australian cents for every rand to discourage the rand leaving South Africa. Because of the limit imposed on us, we decided not to bring our money from the sale of our house but to try and bring it out later.

I longed for what we had left behind and for our house.

During the day, we looked forward to walking down to the post office to use the public phone booth to call our family and friends.

Chris tried his best to encourage me and showered me with love and attention. Sasha happily played with David, oblivious to my unhappiness.

Every day Chris scoured the papers, and checked the noticeboard at social security for job adverts. Little did we know that as a result of the poor economic situation in Australia, unemployment was high. The Liberal Party was clinging to power with Prime Minister Malcolm Fraser at the helm. Jobs were scarce and there were no jobs for electricians in the newspapers. Chris also discovered that he needed to present his papers to the New South Wales Licensing Committee, before he could work. Another delay.

The day Mum arrived, I did not go to the airport to meet her. I tried so hard to be cheerful, but all I wanted to do at that time was pack up and go home. Mum and Frances started spending more and more time together, going out and enjoying themselves, while I fretted in our room.

When Chris received a call from his father to tell him

that Mrs Segers's condition had deteriorated, it was the sign we had been waiting for. His father, faced with having to sell their family home and putting his wife into a nursing home, sounded distressed. Chris felt terribly guilty for having left them behind.

At night, we would lay on our mattress and discuss our return plans. I became resentful of the laughter and fun Mum and Frances were having inside.

'If we must go back, then it's best to do it now, before the baby is born,' Chris said.

'I won't be allowed to fly when I reach seven months.'

'I still feel that we have not given it enough time, but I won't be able to live with myself if I don't go back,' he said. 'It is my duty to help my parents.'

'We must do what is right for us, too,' I said. 'Right now, we are not happy and that is what we must think about.'

We announced our plans to return to South Africa before our baby's due date and before our money ran out. Frances was extremely upset and refused to talk to us. Mum hardly spoke to me, and I felt her disappointment that this was not working out the way she had planned for us all to be together.

When I told Maureen that we were returning, they cancelled their plans to emigrate as well. This upset mum terribly. Her dream was falling apart.

'Mum, you are in holiday mode and we are thinking about our future,' I said when we left for the airport. 'We are very concerned about how long our money will last.'

'You do what you have to do and what makes you happy,' Mum said without looking at me.

I felt so much anger and resented her happiness in

this country. Did she not understand our situation? She knew how comfortably we lived in South Africa, and yet she appeared to be happy with the way Frances lived here.

On our drive to the airport, Frances and her husband spoke to each other while we sat quietly in the back. It felt like the longest drive. Mum stayed home because there was no place for her in the car.

'Where you are going back to, there are black people, brown people and white people,' said David to Sasha.

'Where is that?' asked Sasha.

'Where you live, they have different skin colours,' said David.

My anger rose, but I held back making a comment. Chris held my hand and squeezed it, smiling reassuringly. I looked down at Sasha, so young and so innocent. *What are we doing to her?* My mind raced with things I wanted to say to them, but as we got closer to the airport, all I wanted to do was to board that plane to get home to South Africa and have my baby.

Frances cried as we parted and I held back my tears. Sasha waved her little hand at David as we walked towards the security check-in. I felt drained, confused, and the baby in my belly moved around kicking into my rib cage.

There was so much I wanted to say about the timing of our move to Australia. Frances and her family were not to blame for our failure to make it work. It was our choice to follow them blindly, hoping that our families could be back together again. When I turned to look back, Frances was wiping her tears.

15

HOME CALLING

The long flight home was tiring, and this time there was no exciting adventure waiting for us. We were back to Chris having to find a job and to setting up home again. We were able to stop our furniture from being shipped to Australia and had packed up our household goods to be returned home. Chris discouraged me from calculating how much money we had lost and encouraged me instead to look ahead to the birth of our second baby.

At the DF Malan airport, Mr Segers scooped up Sasha into his arms and smothered her with kisses and cuddles. She laughed and hugged him tightly. I felt tears in my eyes as confusion set in my mind. *What are we doing here?* On our drive home I looked around the streets and, of course, nothing had changed. We passed the shacks in which people were forced to live in poverty, and the mountains lay ahead where white people lived in luxury in separate areas.

I knew already that we had made a mistake to return.

So many thoughts raced through my mind as we drove to Chris's parents' house. We are back in this place that I had wanted to escape from. Nothing had changed here. I still had to cope with the same things I had left behind a mere few months ago—only now, I had a baby growing in my stomach. I was going to give birth and bring another life into this unequal society. Our baby would also be registered as a Cape Coloured and be subjected to the same second-class citizenship as we had been.

I knew Chris felt relieved because his mother's health had deteriorated so quickly, and the relief on his father's face was so clear to see. That evening, after everything had settled down, we made a pact that we would return to Australia in a couple of years.

Chris found a job within a few days of our return and we started making plans to purchase an old house close to where we had lived before. It needed a lot of renovations to make it livable, and thoughts of going back to Australia were soon put on the backburner. We reconnected with our friends and family, and while there were mixed reactions from some, we received great support from our very good friends Charles and Patricia.

On 26 November, after a short labour, Michelin was born at Groote Schuur Hospital. A wide-eyed baby with a thick mop of curls greeted me when the nurse laid him in my arms. I missed sharing this moment with Mum, who was still in Australia. I felt a huge emptiness at not being able to share my joy with her or Frances. I had not seen Maureen, Andy or Georgie since our return. Our family home was empty; Andy lived there while Mum was away but he was always out, and Georgie had moved to George, about six hours drive away. It felt as if our tight-knit family was in tatters. Mum's house, always the centre-piece, the place where we all gathered, now empty.

For the first time, I blamed myself for the split in our family. I felt responsible for Maureen and Andy deciding not to go to Australia, for Mum having to choose between us, for our failure in settling in the new life I had dreamed of; and for encouraging Chris to make these changes.

At my lowest point, Mum surprised me with a visit a week after she had returned from Australia. The atmosphere was cool and an awkwardness hung in the air, but her presence boosted my low mood. She sat cuddling Michelin, but we did not talk about Frances or her holiday in Australia.

Uncertainty about Mum's support for me gnawed at the pit of my stomach. Longing to hear some comforting words and encouragement, Mum's silence pained me. It felt as if Mum was only doing her duty and had come to see her new grandson. I carried the burden in my heart that Mum resented me for changing the plans we had as a family—to follow Frances and her family to Australia.

Our once happy family life now lay in ruins. This weighed heavily on me. Chris encouraged me to talk to Mum about how I felt and to clear the air. I had my opportunity a few weeks later when I visited Mum on my own with Michelin. It was a Saturday afternoon and she was busy with her plants in the back room.

'Mum ...' I said softly, suddenly not sure what I wanted to say.

'Most of my plants died while I was away,' Mum said without looking at me. 'Andy didn't water these plants regularly and now I must re-pot them and start again.'

'How did you enjoy your holiday?' I asked, trying to sound cheerful.

An awkward silence hung in the room as Mum continued potting around in silence. Michelin was asleep in the pram and at that moment I wished he would wake up to give us something to talk about.

'Do you think you did the right thing?' Mum finally asked.

'I wasn't happy, Mum,' I said. I tried to look at her face but she avoided my searching eyes.

'I don't understand it, but if you are happy, then you did the right thing,' she said.

'It may not be the *right* thing, but it was the *best* thing for me, Mum,' I said. 'If only you could have taken our side and looked at how we felt as well. But you always favoured Frances, and would never say anything about her.'

'Favoured Frances? How can you accuse me of favouring one of my children?' Mum said, now glaring at me. 'You children have always said that I favour her, but you are all my children with different wants and needs.'

'Not once in the two months that we lived in the same house over there did you reassure me that everything would be alright,' I screamed. 'Mum, you took sides and left me to sort my own life out.'

'No one could change your mind for you,' she said, her voice remained calm.

'That's not true Mum. The two of you went about enjoying yourselves and you didn't care about me,' I cried.

'I had to make a decision, and I did. I had to let you decide on what's best for you and your family,' she said. 'Now you have a beautiful baby boy and a growing daughter to focus on. In time, it will all become clear to you why you chose this path.'

'But I know you blamed me for the way things turned out. You dreamed of us all going over to Australia and now I ruined it all,' I said.

'Stop blaming yourself.' Mum looked at me, her eyes were filled with tears. 'We all make decisions about our own lives. You had every right to feel the way you did. You must live with it and make peace with your sister.'

Mum showed me a letter from Frances; she was having another baby. I felt the pain of separation even more. She would have shared this news with me as well, but now things were different. I could not share our joy with her and she could not share hers with me. I knew that we had to work out a way forward.

'I am planning to move over there permanently in a year or two,' I heard Mum say while I read the letter.

I spent the next three months trying to cope with Michelin's colic. His incessant screams had me at my wits' end. He was taken off all dairy and put on soy milk, which helped him to settle. The time had also come to make decisions about a school for Sasha, and it really hit us then that we were back to living in our allocated areas and with their allocated schools. We were both determined that she would get the best education that we could afford.

Our options were for Sasha to attend a local coloured school or one of the private Catholic schools which had started to admit coloured and black students in defiance of apartheid a few years earlier. We had heard about St Anne's in Plumstead, a white suburb, and decided to enrol her into that school.

We wanted her to experience life without limitations and this would be the closest we could come to giving her a balanced education. I did not want her to grow up thinking of herself as a second-class citizen, and if this was the way forward, then it was the right decision.

My upbringing was very sheltered and I did not have the opportunity to interact with black or white children. This made me determined that she would experience the freedom I never had.

At our interview with the Deputy Principal, we had so many questions about the process and how things were progressing with students who were already attending the school. The Catholic Church had decided to open all its schools to everyone, and while this was in its infancy, the results so far had been most encouraging.

We were not surprised to learn that they had opposition from some parents and that a small number had already removed their children, not wanting them to integrate. When we received the acceptance letter and announced to some of our family and friends that Sasha would be attending St Anne's, we were also faced with mixed reactions.

Some questioned our motives and what we hoped to gain from her attending a white school, and others questioned our approval of the quota system (which the Catholic schools, unlike most other private schools, actually ignored). We remained determined that Sasha should be exposed to interacting with all races and that she would not be subjected to the rules and laws under which we had grown up.

A few months after we had returned from Australia, Mr Segers sold their house and moved in with his sister. Mrs Segers, who was completely bed-ridden, went into a nursing home. We bought a house in the same area where we lived before. The house was old and in need of renovations, but it was all we could afford. I was home with Michelin, who was only three months old, and Sasha was at school. It felt as if we were making progress with settling back in.

Sasha settled into the new school with ease and the other parents were friendly and welcoming. Soon she was attending parties of children from all race groups. We also noticed that Sasha did not identify children by colour as we so easily did in our conversations. She thought that Lucy, a little girl in her class, lived in the white suburb of Claremont, because she travelled on the train with some classmates. Little did Sasha know that Lucy sat in a different carriage and then had to board a bus to the township further away.

Travelling on the train presented huge complications when children had to go on excursions because they had to sit in different carriages, as identified by race. Undeterred, the school asked parents to drive the kids on school excursions to ensure that they would not be segregated. Whenever I dropped Sasha off at school, I would watch with such pride as her friends of all races welcomed her. She was still oblivious to this coloured label we were raised under.

Renovating our new home was exciting and gave me a focus during the many days I wrestled with my emotions.

Whenever Mum showed me pictures of Frances's baby girl, Leanne, and kept me up-to-date with their news, I thought of writing to Frances. We had not been in contact since our departure from Australia, and that weighed heavily on my mind.

Georgie had finally settled down in George and married a woman whom none of us had met. She was pregnant and expecting his first child. Maureen also announced that she was pregnant with her second baby.

'The Crosher dynasty is growing so fast,' I said to Mum. 'You will soon have to open a crèche for all your grandchildren.'

'I told you that I will be leaving soon to settle in Australia,' she reminded me.

'I know you want to be with Frances,' I snapped. 'You have all of us here and yet that is where you want to be.'

'This life is not for me,' Mum said. 'After looking at how well the older people are looked after in Australia, I know that is what I want.'

'Family is everything, Mum,' I said. 'But as you told me, you do what will make you happy.'

'This is no life for me. I sacrificed my whole life for you children, and I did it with every ounce of my being. Now this is my time and I want you all to be happy for me,' she said.

Whenever I had these conversations with Mum, my thoughts would go back to us moving to Australia. I knew that it was not possible at this stage, but it was something we had at the back of our minds.

'Do you still think we did the right thing?' I would ask Chris from time to time.

'Don't fret too much about it now,' Chris would

brush it aside whenever I raised the topic.

He spent so much time working and renovating our home, and I was left home with the children. I started yearning to go back to work or to do something other than child-minding.

Whenever Chris came home with disturbing stories of racial discrimination, I was dismayed that we returned to what I was so eager to get away from. One day he was clearly distressed by what he had witnessed. On weekends he took on extra work to make additional money, since my being home to take care of Sasha and Michelin was putting a strain on our budget.

Chris was doing the electrical installation on a house in Claremont. The owner had several people working on the project. To get cheap labour, the builder would go to a road in Philippi, a popular place where desperate black labourers congregated. Chris told me how the men would jump on the back of the *bakkie* (pick-up truck) to do a day's work.

It was compulsory for blacks to carry an identity document in the form of a passbook which permitted them to live and work in Cape Town. Most of the labourers waiting in that area had no passbooks. It was illegal for a black person to be outside the homelands or designated black area without a passbook.

As the work day ended, Chris was packing up his tools when he heard loud voices and saw some of the black labourers running past him. Two police vans were coming up the road towards them.

Behind him, he heard glass crashing and chaos ensued as police set chase after the labourers who scattered in different directions. Chris followed the builder to inspect the crashing sound. They discovered the newly-installed glass window on the upper floor smashed, and shards of glass on the ground. The builder walked back to his van and continued loading his equipment.

A trail of blood led Chris to where a man had collapsed behind a pile of dirt. He propped the man up and led him to a place behind some bricks. There Chris helped him stop the bleeding. With blood pouring out of a gash in the man's leg, Chris strapped it with some strips torn from a shirt.

'The man was so anxious and his eyes darted about. He didn't have a passbook and he knew that if he was caught, he would be taken to jail,' Chris said sadly. 'He was prepared to risk his life by jumping through a glass window.'

He sat quietly for a long while before he told me the rest of the story.

'Two labourers were caught and were taken away in the police van, and the others managed to get away,' he said. 'None of the men who fled received payment for the day's work.'

The man with the leg injury refused to go to hospital, so Chris drove him back to where he had been picked up. Chris gave him some money and the man gave profuse thanks.

'I suspect that either the owner or the builder called the police,' he said. 'Towards the end of the day, knowing that these workers did not have passbooks, they took the evil way out.'

Like these workers, our parents lived this way and did so without malice towards the government. For most of them, carving out a decent standard of living for their families was more important than fighting the regime.

As much as I tried to shift these stories to the back of my mind, they remained stark reminders of why we had left South Africa. We were still lost in this society. The government still had a firm grip on the country, despite mounting international sanctions and pressure.

I had a yearning to talk to Frances but I could not get myself to write to her. I had seen recent letters that she wrote to Maureen in which she expressed her anger and resentment towards me for leaving. She blamed me for influencing everyone else from going to Australia. I decided against contacting her.

Michelin had been experiencing constant colds and congestion ever since his first birthday. It had worsened in the winter months. Dad had been afflicted with asthma and with Chris also suffering the disease, I was fearful that Michelin would befall the same fate. When his diagnosis was confirmed, along with many allergies, I was shattered and fearful that he would suffer as Dad had. He was also found to be allergic to penicillin, leaving few options for him to be treated for infections.

I set out to change Michelin's diet and began eliminating processed food and whatever else I was told would lead to improved health. His health improved with the new diet, however he would have sporadic asthma attacks. The paediatrician, a Dutchman, who managed his condition assured us that if managed properly there was every likelihood that he would outgrow this condition by the time he started school.

I carried the paediatrician's card with me, and a few times I had to call him after-hours for advice on how to deal with Michelin's wheezing chest. He was one of a group of doctors who had a private ward at Victoria Hospital in Wynberg, where patients of all races were admitted.

One Saturday during the winter of 1984, Michelin was having breathing difficulties and his condition worsened as the day progressed. He had been unwell for a few days and the medication the local doctor had prescribed was not effective. I called the after-hours number on the paediatrician's card to seek his advice.

'Bring him to Victoria Hospital,' he said. 'It will be best for me to examine him and then decide whether to admit him. Pack a bag and meet me at the back entrance.'

'That is where the white entrance is,' Chris said. 'Did you tell him who you are? He must be making a mistake.'

When we arrived at the hospital, the doctor was waiting near the door and ushered us into the white entrance. Both Chris and I were unsure about entering, thinking that the doctor was making a mistake. We followed him, with Chris carrying Michelin in his arms and me holding Sasha's hand. My eyes scanned the emergency room: seven empty beds and in the far corner a white patient lay asleep. Everything looked spotless; two hospital orderlies were sitting at the reception desk.

'Doctor, who is the patient?' one orderly asked, looking at us and then turning his attention back to the doctor.

'I need a bed to examine my patient,' said the doctor.

'If *this* is your patient, Doctor, then you are on the wrong side,' the orderly smiled, pointing the way to the coloured side.

'All I want to do is examine this little boy to decide whether to admit him in my ward,' the doctor said.

'But I am telling Doctor that you are on the wrong side. Please follow that corridor and it will take you to the coloured side,' the orderly said adamantly.

Throwing his hands in the air, the doctor grabbed his bag and told us to follow him down the corridor.

Cursing about the difficulties in this country, the doctor led the way down the corridor to the coloured emergency ward. We walked in silence behind him, Chris holding Michelin upright to ease his cough and Sasha holding my hand.

Chaos awaited us as the doors swung open in the coloured emergency room. Crowded with patients, sitting and standing in the ward, every bed filled. The medical staff were run off their feet attending to the many patients. There was not an empty bed in sight. Victoria Hospital was the closest hospital for coloured people living in the southern suburbs.

Approaching the desk, the doctor asked, 'Where can I examine my patient, please?' An exasperated orderly looked at the doctor and then at us. Throwing his hands in the air, he said, 'You tell me where, Doctor? We don't have place for another body in this ward. You will have to wait.'

Clearly frustrated, the doctor motioned us to follow him back down the corridor to the white emergency room. At this stage, Michelin was coughing and struggling to breathe.

'This country ...' the doctor said, his voice trailing off as if he did not want to say too much. 'If I am not allowed to examine him in this ward, you will have to take him straight to admissions in my private ward.'

Chris was ready to launch into an attack if anyone

refused Michelin a bed. His jaw tightened and his breath quickened. With the doctor leading the way, we marched into the empty white ward and without consulting anyone, the doctor walked across to a bed. The orderlies came rushing but stopped dead in their tracks when they saw our faces. From across the room they started protesting and threatening us with the police.

'You do that,' the doctor said. 'You call the police and they will have to arrest me for examining this sick child.'

Running across the room to the far corner, they drew the curtains around the elderly white patient and continued to pace about the ward, waiting for us to finish.

I looked at Sasha where she stood next to the bed, watching the doctor examine her little brother. She was so innocent, and unaware that these people were judging us as second-class citizens, not good enough to be examined in their ward. These were ordinary people like us, but they had the power to refuse entry into what they were told was their side of the public hospital. Because they had white skin.

A nurse appeared and walked over towards us to inquire what we were doing on this side. In silence, the doctor continued to examine Michelin, ignoring her questioning. That night Michelin was admitted into his private ward where he slept in a bed next to white children. There was no fuss, no one cared. Parents were worried about their sick children, and not interested in politics.

This humiliation of being treated as second-class citizens was now reaching our children and that was harder to deal with. *How could these people see themselves as better than us?* These workers in hospitals and other public places carried out the law to the last letter and continued to vote to keep this government in power. By having the vote, they could keep apartheid alive. They could make the choice to be superior to us.

These human beings had the authority to approve whether our son's skin colour allowed him entry into the emergency room, as if his skin would tarnish their sheets. They could chase us away like they would a stray who came through the door. We were all born into this, four generations of my family grew up this way and accepted this as our fate.

But these whites were people just like us, with hearts and souls. *Why could they not see that this was wrong?* Things had to change and *they* had the power to do so. While we had a small victory that night, we still had an insurmountable mountain to climb before we would reach equality.

Because of Mum and her determination, we could leave this country and start afresh elsewhere so that our children would not be subjected to the treatment dished out by this government.

'We must start thinking about going back to Australia,' I said that night as we sat at Michelin's bedside in the hospital. 'I know we tried before, but this time we must do our own research and plan things better. I know we can make it work.'

Chris nodded. He leaned over to kiss Michelin before taking Sasha home, leaving me to stay the night. I knew things were tough for Chris; his mother's health was failing and his father had also been admitted to hospital a couple of times over the previous few months.

Later that year, Mrs Segers passed away peacefully in the nursing home. Her death, while not unexpected, was difficult for Mr Segers. They had been married for 40 years and his health was also deteriorating rapidly. This put an added strain on Chris, who worried about his father's decline, renovating the house and my constant nagging about our future.

Sasha, who enjoyed school and participated in extramural activities, remained shy and quietly spoken. To help her social skills we enrolled her in a swimming programme and she excelled at it. She adored Michelin and they were inseparable from a young age. Sasha's long curly hair attracted attention wherever we went.

One of the days that really tested my patience with raising two children became a turning point in my way forward. I knew that I had to find something to do. It was during the school holidays and I had spent the day spring-cleaning. Sasha and Michelin were playing around the house. When I returned to the kitchen, I found Michelin in a pool of cooking oil. Unable to reach him because of the slippery floor, I had to cover the floor with sheets and drag him towards me. After cleaning up the mess, I stood at the kitchen window to witness Sasha hosing down my lines of dry laundry. I knew that the time had come to make a change.

While I enjoyed motherhood, I yearned to do something more with my life. With Sasha at school and me home alone with Michelin, I felt stifled. My brain needed stimulation. Most of my friends living in the area worked or studied.

To fill in my days, I got more involved in our parish, and when an opportunity came to be part of the committee to arrange the first Debutante Ball, I jumped at the chance. For the rest of the year, my mind was occupied with raising funds and supporting the debutantes.

Mum left for Australia at the end of that year. She showed the same determination as she had when we were growing up. She had worked full-time and sold clothing to neighbours and friends to earn additional money. Now she had made up her mind that her future lay in Australia. This left me pondering our future and Mum's dream of us all living together in Australia. I knew that Maureen and Andy would follow, but Georgie had no interest.

Chris had started growing closer to his birth mother and her family. He began spending more time with them, which caused Mr Segers a great deal of insecurity. He worried that Sasha and Michelin would grow more attached to Chris's birth mother. While both Chris and his mother struggled to build a relationship, he grew closer to his new-found siblings. He enjoyed visiting them and we started spending more time with them as a family.

Chris was looking for answers from her as to why she gave him up for adoption and who his birth father was. No answers were forthcoming.

When Mr Segers died on the anniversary of Mrs Segers's death, I knew that Chris would finally be relieved of the guilt he had felt about leaving them and taking Sasha and Michelin away. Mr Segers's death was a huge blow to Sasha who was very attached to her grandfather and often spent a few days with him during school holidays.

I gave Chris some time to come to terms with the loss of his father before raising the topic of emigration again.

16

STATELESS AND FLAGLESS

Sydney, Australia: August 1988, Late Winter

Almost exactly six years after we had first come to Australia in July 1982, our plane touched down in Sydney. This second time our mood was upbeat. We had not announced our return, so I was excited about surprising Mum, but apprehensive about a reunion with Frances. We had not spoken to each other since our last hasty departure. I had spoken to Mum regularly over the years but my conversations with Frances had been limited to greetings and polite inquiries. Because of the separation, we had unfinished discussions and I knew that she would be relentless in her pursuit to clear the air.

Mum, who was living with Frances, had left South Africa three years prior to settle permanently in Australia.

As the cab made its way along the streets towards Liverpool, where Frances and her family lived, I recognised some of the landmarks. It was a cold, rainy morning.

Chris, in his usual manner, questioned the driver about the route he took. Then we arrived at Frances's house.

'No, no, this is not true,' shouted Mum from the doorway as we climbed out of the cab.

'Frances, come quickly,' she called out over her shoulder as she rushed towards us.

Scooping Sasha and Michelin into her arms, she smothered them with kisses. 'Look how much you've grown,' she said, as she touched their faces and hugged them.

In the doorway stood Frances, motionless, watching as Mum hugged us and helped carry our luggage inside. I was unsure of the reception, but when I approached Frances, tears streamed down her face as she hugged me. All the hurtful comments, accusations and blame for our failed first attempt at settling in Australia washed away.

'You should have told us that you were coming,' she said. 'Mum could have had a heart attack. We thought something was odd when Mum called Maureen to ask why your phone was disconnected. Maureen's response was very vague.'

I breathed a sigh of relief. The part that I had dreaded the most, the reunion, was now behind us. We had planned to find a motel close by and to stay there until our planned departure for Brisbane, but Mum and Frances would not hear of it. They started stripping beds and rearranging bedrooms to accommodate us.

We met Leanne, six months younger than Michelin, for the first time. The cousins hit it off instantly and soon the adults were left to catch up lost years.

I was apprehensive about breaking the news to Mum that we would not be staying in Sydney. I felt as if I had given her a moment of happiness and then snatched it away in one quick swoop.

'We've looked at the Brisbane housing market and it is definitely more affordable for us,' I explained to Mum. 'We must make it work this time. And, you will have somewhere else to visit as well.'

'Brisbane is not that far away,' she said smiling. 'You must do what is best for your lives. And, besides that, if you don't like it there, you can drive back.'

Our experience in Brisbane taught us once again that our lives can be turned upside down, no matter how well we've prepared. We had arrived during Expo '88, when everyone in Brisbane was in holiday mode. The work was not as plentiful as we had heard. Two days after our arrival, during breakfast at our motel, Chris read the *Sydney Morning Herald*'s job section and found several electrician's jobs in Sydney. When he called to inquire about the jobs, they asked him to send his resume immediately. We used the motel's fax machine and within a couple of hours he had secured three interviews.

So we did exactly as Mum had said in her parting words: we hired a car and drove the 930 kilometres down the coast back to Sydney.

It all felt like one great adventure for us. We were still in holiday mode and consciously continued to encourage each other to stay positive. Sasha and Michelin enjoyed the sights along the way. We stopped at the Big Pineapple in Woombye. We bought fresh fruit, and spent the night at Coffs Harbour to take in more of that seaside city. We knew that we would have to enrol the children in school as soon as we arrived in Sydney.

Two weeks after Chris secured a job, we moved into

a rented house in Heckenberg, in the south-western suburbs. Sasha and Michelin were enrolled in the local Catholic school, and I found a part-time job at a small family
company close to home. I was happy to be reconciled
with Frances and Mum's happiness was contagious.

Our family rift had been mended. We were ticking
the boxes; our life was finally falling into place.

To further add to our joy, Maureen called to say that
they had been accepted and would be arriving in Australia in a few months' time. Mum's dream was slowly
becoming a reality. Frances and her family, the pioneers,
had opened the way for us all to think about our future.
Without their bold decision to leave South Africa, we
would still have been travelling in segregated carriages
and Mum would still have been living in the council housing estate.

My thoughts often turned to our many friends and
family we had left behind. In the first few months I made
many phone calls to hear their voices and to appease
myself that we made the right decision. After the flurry
of activity in setting up our home, settling the children in
school, finding jobs and getting to know our surroundings, I started suffering pangs of homesickness for my old
life.

I longed for our church community where I had produced so many plays and fundraising events. Whenever I
walked into our new parish, nobody knew me. After Mass
there was no one to talk to, and everyone just went on
their way. I was reaching that same point as a few years
ago, when I had felt lost, when those feelings of not
belonging started to creep in.

I didn't want to worry Chris with these feelings of

insecurity and kept them to myself. I was determined to connect to find my place in this society. I had to.

That connection came when we attended our first Australia Day celebration at Darling Harbour. It was a spur-of-the-moment decision to take the train into the city and join the crowds for the celebration.

I watched how Sasha and Michelin held on to their small Australian flags as we walked around the harbour. The crowds grew larger as the time for the fireworks display neared. We had the perfect vantage point on the steps facing the tall buildings. Before 9 pm a laser beamed the Australian flag onto one of the tall buildings. People cheered and boisterously broke out into singing the anthem. I didn't know the words of the anthem; I knew the words to *Die Stem*, the South African anthem. Only, I never sang that anthem; we had stopped singing it at school when I was about ten years old. I had never held a South African flag either.

I thought back to primary school and how we stood at the flagpole during assembly to watch the raising of the flag and to sing the Afrikaans national anthem. Dad, heavily opposed to anything to do with the government, forbade us to sing it. The words of *Die Stem* did not fairly represent the nation. The flag was a symbol of our oppression. The orange, white and blue colours were a constant reminder of the racist government and what they stood for.

Now, looking around Darling Harbour, I observed the sea of people singing loudly, some draped in the flag and others waving it. In front of me stood Sasha and Michelin, smiling at each other as they waved their flag.

What had they done to us in South Africa?

They deprived us of feeling attached to our own country, to our own anthem, to our own flag. I was part of a whole generation which grew up devoid of allegiance to our sovereignty. Never had I felt so strongly to belong, to place my hand on my heart and belt out the anthem, to adorn myself with such pride in a flag.

17

LITTLE COLOURED BOY

A year after we came to Australia, Maureen and her family arrived. We decided to move to the southern suburbs to be closer to the city. I was successful in getting an administrative position in the New South Wales State Government in The Cabinet Office, a secretariat providing policy advice to the Premier's Office. I was in awe of where I found myself. I had the freedom to walk on the same floor as the Premier of New South Wales. In South Africa, jobs like these were available only to white workers.

In 1992, Premier Nick Greiner was forced to resign. On his last day, he walked through The Cabinet Office, shaking the hand of every employee. People were so moved, as he made his way around the floor that we broke into spontaneous applause.

A few months later I took up a role in the newly-established Natural Resources Unit where I worked with some amazing women establishing themselves as leaders in the policy area. I was quickly building up my reputation through hard work and dedication to my role.

When we arrived in Australia, we had promised each other that we would give ourselves five years to settle down and then return to South Africa for a holiday. Georgie and Andy were still living in South Africa. Georgie was now divorced and the father of a nine-year-old daughter, Fiola. Andy was married with three children: Cindy, Chad and Bradley. We kept in regular phone contact but I started longing to see them.

Meanwhile, we bought our first house and set about renovating the property. Chris had changed his mind about returning to South Africa, preferring to spend the money on the house. I decided to take Sasha and Michelin along on the trip.

We spent three glorious weeks catching up with everyone. I saw Georgie almost every day of the three weeks. Sasha and Michelin both contracted chicken pox on the trip which meant that we had to stay an additional ten days. This gave me more time and the kids got to know their uncle very well. He tried to brush off my worrying questions about his excessive drinking.

When it was time to leave, Andy promised that he would apply to come to live in Australia within the next year. Georgie and I made plans for him to surprise Mum with a visit at the end of that year.

After my return home to Australia, I called Georgie several times to plan his surprise visit. I was in total shock when Andy called to tell us that Georgie had been admitted to hospital in a serious condition. I called a local priest, the hospital chaplain, who promised to visit him straight away. I was numb with shock when the priest called me back. His words stayed on my mind. *Your brother is an alcoholic and he is gravely ill.*

Mum, Frances, Maureen and I couldn't believe it. We were hoping that he would recover in hospital and would be released soon.

The next evening, Chris was working late. After dinner and when Sasha and Michelin had gone to bed, I also fell asleep, exhausted. Startled, I woke up two hours later. I felt this sudden urge to talk to Georgie and decided to call the hospital. The nurse's voice, hesitant and unsure, had me repeating my name. A few moments of silence, and finally I heard a male voice introduce himself. From somewhere in the distance I heard a voice.

'Did I hear someone say something about Georgie?'

'Yes, I am his sister.'

'I am sorry, but your brother just died,' I heard the voice say. 'But hold on, your other brother is here.'

Andy had felt that same restlessness while he was at work and decided to go to the hospital. He stood at Georgie's bedside at the very moment that our brother died. And I was on the other end of the phone at that very moment. I spoke to Andy for a few moments. He was in shock.

I sat in the dark room for a while. *How could Andy cope on his own?* I dialled Frances' number. Her screams shot through the earpiece when I told her the news. She dropped the phone. I sat listening to her cry, waiting for her to pick up the phone again. After a while I disconnected and called Maureen who became hysterical and also dropped the phone. Again, I sat in the dark room holding the phone, listening to her cry. *Should I call Mum now or wait until morning?*

The sound of Chris pulling into the drive way distracted me. A little while later the doorbell rang. It was Frances. We stood hugging each other. When the doorbell rang again, it was Maureen. Tears streamed down her face as we hugged. Together we went to tell Mum the news.

Two days later, we flew out to bury Georgie.

A month later, Andy came for a visit. He had decided to come to Australia with his family. We were overjoyed to have him here. Mum immediately started planning for his arrival, even though it was a year away.

In March 1995, Labor won the State election and I was offered a secondment to work in the Office of the Hon. Kim Yeadon MP as a parliamentary coordinator.

Life was good for us. We were renovating our first home, Sasha, now in Year 12, was an accomplished swimmer and had won many accolades for her swimming prowess. She had grown into a fine young lady with a firm determination to succeed. She had saved up her money from a part-time job to buy her first car.

We were saving and planning for a trip around the world. These were the things we had dreamed of in South Africa, but it felt impossible to achieve while living there.

Michelin, sporty and musical, had been accepted into Year 7 at St Mary's Cathedral College, not very far from where my office was. His adventurous nature had us visiting the hospital emergency many times for his escapades. A spate of fractures, stitches and bruises were all reminders of his childhood. For the first few months he would come to my office after school so that we could travel home on the train.

Several feisty young Labor colleagues worked in the

office. It made for an interesting work environment. My skills and knowledge of the administrative processes that are involved in presenting new legislation before Parliament secured me the role in the Ministerial Office.

Fast-paced and challenging, the office was an exciting environment. I was still in awe at times at where I found myself. Whenever I entered Parliament House and some of the staff knew me by name, a huge sense of pride filled my being. Working in a small multi-disciplinary team, it often was all hands on deck, working long hours during Parliamentary Sitting times.

My first flight on a small plane with the Minister to an event in rural New South Wales was something to behold. No one knew how proud I felt sitting behind the Minister, the Chief of Staff and a journalist. People treated me with the utmost respect as I liaised about the logistics for the event and the Minister's speech. No one cared about the colour of my skin. They listened when I talked, they asked my advice about my area of expertise, I was a valued worker.

What appeared to be an ordinary day in their working lives, for me—a girl from the council housing estate on the Cape Flats—it felt surreal.

We could not wait to relinquish our South African citizenship. Exactly two years after our arrival, we had applied for Australian citizenship and voted for a New South Wales government for the first time in 1991.

In 1997, a friendly and outgoing receptionist started in our office. We often exchanged conversations about general topics. One afternoon she was at the front desk when Michelin arrived after school.

The next day she asked me about him: age, school,

name etc. She repeated the pronunciation of his name several times to get it right and remarked how suited it was to a little coloured boy.

Did she really call Michelin a little coloured boy?

Stunned, I walked back to my office. The longer I thought about it, the more incensed I became. I was even more unsettled when some of my colleagues showed signs of awkwardness when they heard about the comment. In my office, I raged and cursed.

This is my son.

What made him look like a little coloured boy? Was it his sunburnt skin colour, his curly hair or his dark brown eyes? Couldn't she see that he was sunburnt? He had curly hair but it wasn't coarse. He had smooth bouncy curls.

That was the same tag stamped on my forehead when I was born. Little coloured girl. I felt a rage beating in my arms down to my hands.

I wanted to lash out to protect my child from this vile tag. I had lived with it and being coloured determined the way I grew up. A second-class citizen. We came to Australia because I wanted to make sure that he grew up just a boy like his many friends. He played the oboe in the school orchestra. On the basketball court, he was a star player who earned the tag 'Minister of Defence'. We taught him to respect everyone.

No one called him *a little coloured boy*.

Penny Wong, later a Senator, was a policy advisor to the Minister at the time. One of my colleagues told her about the incident and how upset I was. She called me to the meeting room to discuss the incident. I became extremely emotional as I explained how I felt about the comment. *Was I overreacting?* Since arriving in Australia,

I had felt welcomed everywhere I went. We blended into the community. No one seemed to care about the colour of my skin. I no longer felt vulnerable. How wrong I was.

Penny was warm and comforting. She told me about her own experiences of growing up, how she was called all sorts of names and not accepted. We sat talking for a while and she offered me some comfort and words of encouragement. I was disappointed that no one else in the office talked about it. Didn't they understand that it was an offensive statement?

Future young political leaders appeared awkward and shirked away from discussing it. Except for Erika, a young mother who expressed her dismay at the insensitive remark. She was of Hungarian background and bore the brunt of racism against migrants in the 1970s in Australia. She understood. I wanted to confront the receptionist. I wanted her to be reprimanded and even sacked, but nothing happened.

That evening, I talked to Chris. He told me to stand up for myself by confronting her and let her know how I felt. When I approached her desk the next morning, she greeted me excitedly. Before I could say a word, she handed me some photographs of her family.

Her partner was Pacific Islander and next to him stood a little boy who looked very similar to Michelin. I smiled and looked at her beaming face. She remarked how similar the boys looked. Clearly excited for me to see her family, I stopped short of telling her what was on my mind. I felt awkward—she had referred to her husband and little boy as coloured.

It was clearly her issue and her way of identifying them. She saw their skin colour as different to hers. I realised that she would not see the reference as offensive. But, I wondered what issues she had with race and how she saw other people. The difference was that it was her own decision to refer to her son as a little coloured boy. It wasn't legislated, as it had been under apartheid. That was the difference.

I never had that conversation with her.

Back in my office, I touched my skin as it glowed in the sunlight streaming into my office. The hairs on my arm gleamed in the sunlight. I touched both arms and felt the smoothness of my skin. It was a darker shade of pale.

For the first time, I felt a connection with my skin. It was something to be proud of, to be comfortable with. In South Africa many coloured and black women used a cream to try and lighten their skin. A fair skin signified a connection to a white heritage and could open doors to a better life.

I felt the pain of my ancestors who had suffered the degradation of being classified as second-class citizens, purely based on the colour of their skin.

In South Africa, that opened the door to riches or closed it and booted us into poverty.

That reference, little coloured boy, should never be acceptable in society. It still haunts me that I did not confront her to explain my feelings. But I also realised how apartheid damaged me, and for any healing to take place I had to love my skin and let go of the past.

Now references to my multi-cultural heritage stirs memories of pride in a people who rose above adversity. I am a descendant of people born in and out of Africa with the spirit of the Bantu farm workers and iron smiths, the rich tapestry of Afro-Indo-Sino cultures of the Saints of Saint Helena; and a European-craftsmen who settled with a farmer's kitchen maid. Together they helped to build the nation where I come from. Their spirit is in my soul.

This is who I am.

DEAR DAD,

I have so much to tell you about the many things you missed out on. I know that you would have marvelled at the many changes that happened in South Africa and around the world. While writing this letter to you, I am filled with waves of emotions: from sadness, to joy, to laughter and tears.

You never had the privilege of becoming a homeowner in your lifetime. But I know that you would have been happy for Mum when she became the homeowner of 76 Pickerill Street. She worked so hard all her life to keep that roof over our heads. In a surprise move, the Housing Department decided to transfer ownership of houses to long-term tenants. That house holds so many happy memories of you, Dad. It is also the house where you took your last breath.

You told us that after you moved from St Helena, your birthplace, you could have gone to England, Australia or Canada. Well, we did what you didn't do. We are all grown up and have our own families. Frances and her family were the first ones to leave South Africa and the rest of us followed her to set up home in Australia. You now have Australian-born grandchildren and 15 great-grandchildren. You can be content that they have grown up free of law enforced racial discrimination. I know how much you wished that for us.

Four of your great-grandchildren are mine: two girls, Chelsea Latai and Charlotte Lisia, and two boys, Joshua Benjamin and Alexander Christian. They are the future, borne from the tree of life that you and Mum planted in that housing estate. They are our hope for the future and will go forth and spread their branches to fill a forest that belongs to you and Mum.

At the time when you talked about Nelson Mandela, I was too young to grasp his significance. I am so glad that you were wrong about Nelson Mandela dying in prison. Because he didn't, Dad. He rose above his incarcerators and became President of South Africa and steered the country out of the dark days of apartheid.

I could tell you, that the *end* of apartheid in South Africa happened as you had predicted. But that would sound as if it was easy. It did not happen because of the self-destruction within the Nationalist government, as you had hoped. It happened because of the relentless uprising of the youth in South

Africa and economic sanctions from the international community strangled the hold the government had on the country. The economic sanctions crippled the country, and forced the government to relinquish power. It was so moving Dad, the whole world rallied in support of releasing Nelson Mandela.

But, the fight for freedom came at a price. There were many deaths and innocent people caught in the cross-fire. Throughout that, the government remained relentless in holding a firm grip on the country. Our streets were burning like you couldn't imagine. Political activists disappeared, some never to be seen again; students and innocent bystanders were brutally shot and killed by the police in the name of upholding the law.

However, with the pressure from the international community, the government had no choice but to release Nelson Mandela and to begin restitution. The time had come for them and their supporters to share the wealth and privilege that they had benefitted from all those years. The Group Areas Act and all those other divisive and degrading laws that you so despised were abolished.

While we didn't get to experience the historic transformation in South Africa, we watched from afar, as television networks around the world beamed a victorious Nelson Mandela walking through the gates of Victor Verster Prison to freedom. What a moment in our history that was! When President Mandela visited Sydney on his world tour, we joined thousands of people on the streets to catch a glimpse of him.

Things are so different now, Dad. Advances in technology allow people to have a voice and it can be carried around the world in seconds. The freedom of speech which we were denied is now a right, and people are using it free of recriminations. There are people who will never know what it felt like to be silenced out of fear.

I know you would have punched the air to know that rugby union played a role in the dismantling of apartheid. In 1977 the Commonwealth leaders signed the Gleneagles Agreement, to oppose apartheid in the strongest terms by expelling South Africa from all international competition.

The only country to break that agreement was the New Zealand rebel team which agreed to play the all-white Springbok team. I wish you could have seen the reaction of the rest of the world. In an act of defiance, Australian Prime Minister Malcolm Fraser refused landing rights to the plane carrying the Springboks en-route to New Zealand. Australians and New Zealanders took to the playing field to vehemently protest the all-white Springboks.

With the National Party government maintaining its segregation policies, every sportsperson and sports fan in South Africa suffered. The government and the voters were responsible for prolonging the agony.

I wish we had talked more, especially about the many things that impacted our existence in those dark days. I will never really know if you would have been happy with the changes in South Africa today.

One thing I do know is, that you would have called for all those sporting statistics to be scratched and restarted. You would have said that those records held by white sports-people do not reflect the true talent in South Africa. They were rated as the best only because they were measured against their white peers. Sometimes in the silence, I can hear your voice protesting.

Dad, one of the saddest times for me was a week after you died, your beloved Lions rugby team thrashed the Springboks in the third test in Port Elizabeth. I missed your smiling face next to the red wireless when Philip scored a drop-kick in the third test. Who can forget your jubilation when star player Philip Bennett scored that 50-yard try in the second test. The fourth test ended in a draw, just short of the white-wash you were hoping for.

You will be happy to know that I haven't lost my passion for cricket and rugby—it's like a piece of you I hold so dear. We talk about you so often, when I tell your grandchildren how passionate you were about sport and about your wry sense of humour. Our lives are so vastly different since we moved to Australia 30 years ago. And we now support the Wallabies, another one of your teams.

And Dad, you never lived to see the many historic moments. South Africa hosted the 1995 Rugby World Cup and their first Cricket World Cup. That anthem *Die Stem* and the flag, symbols of oppression had died. We watched on television as the strains of the new anthem, *Nkosi Sikelel' iAfrika*, filled Newlands Stadium, the bright colours of the new flag were adorned around the people of the new Rainbow Nation. It was a sight to behold.

Would you have cheered for the Springboks at the 1995 Rugby World Cup shortly after apartheid was dismantled? I am left to ponder this thought.

I am yet to visit Newlands Stadium to watch a sporting match. I remember how strongly you felt about the racial divide in sport. Despite your passion for cricket and rugby, you refused to go to the stadium because you had to use the non-white separate entrance and the standing room allocation. The little red wireless allowed you to visualise the game.

South Africans are free now and there is already a generation of 'born frees', young people who will thankfully never know about legislated discrimination.

Do you remember how many times I got into trouble for entertaining the others by dancing in the dark when we should have been sleeping? You always smiled when I was bursting with excitement about producing my own backyard concerts. You would watch as I set up the performance space, using a blanket thrown over the washing line to hide the stage from my audience made up of neighbourhood children.

Well, Dad, I know you will be proud that I now produce concerts on proper stages for people who buy tickets to my shows. Yes, my own shows in theatres and iconic entertainment venues around Australia and New Zealand.

Moving to Australia opened many doors and opportunities for all of us. We've been able to travel to the many places we talked about. We were also finally able to watch the Olympic Games live on television. But the highlight for me, something that brought tears to my eyes, was when I worked as part of the Medal Ceremonies team for the Sydney 2000 Olympic Games and the Paralympics Games. Yes Dad, me, the girl from the Cape Flats, made it to the world stage.

St Helena, your birthplace, has also gone through a transformation. It now has an airport and people travel there in search of their ancestry. That is the one thing I regret not talking to you about. I know you didn't want to recall your childhood memories, but I wish that you would have told us more about where you were born and what you remembered about your parents.

Whenever I hear about St Helena, I feel a connection to you. My imagination runs wild and I visualise the place where you would have walked the streets. I hope to visit your birthplace so that I can breathe in my rich ancestry—and to find a piece of you.

Mum is doing well and has been blessed with a long life. She has devoted her life to us. But you would have known that is what she would do. Andy carries a strong resemblance to you and your grandson Michelin has the same mass of unruly curls. And Maureen, she is your girl of great courage. Thrust into adulthood so young, she was strong enough to rise above it and to free herself from the pain and suffering she endured and is now leading a fulfilling life.

We started off as a family of eight and now there are four of us left. We often talk about you, Owen, Georgie and Frances. All I have are my memories of you and them. Such precious memories that I cling to when I feel sad about you all leaving. Please, tell them that I love and miss them, especially Owen who spent such a short time with us.

Growing up, you and I had such special moments, Dad, and many conversations where you came close to revealing stories of your childhood. I hope you know that I carry with me the things you taught me about life and standing up for myself. It's the fibre woven into my being. I have reached into that vault many times to sustain me during challenging times.

Even though I left South Africa many years ago, I can never forget my roots, Dad. The roots that you and Mum planted in South Africa, it lies buried within my soul.

I never got to say goodbye or to express my love and gratitude to you. I know that you loved us in your own very special way.

I cherish your memories Dad,

Beryl

ABOUT THE AUTHOR

Beryl Crosher-Segers was born in Cape Town, South Africa, in 1955, seven years after the reigning National Party imposed the system of apartheid. Through her mixed heritage she was classified as coloured.

In addition to her writing, Beryl is the Founder of One World Community Arts Network, a community project celebrating cultural diversity, and is the owner of C Major Events, an entertainment business. Beryl's background is administration in government. She is also impassioned by fundraising.

Beryl is a highly-regarded community representative. Her awards include the Celebrate African-Australia's Captain's Award for service to the South African Community and a Human Rights Award from the University of Technology, Sydney.

Beryl resides in Sydney, Australia, with her husband, daughter, son, and grandchildren.

Beryl Crosher-Segers is available for bookings for presentations, workshops, live events, conferences, gatherings and book-signings.

Follow Beryl at:

www.berylcroshersegers.com
facebook.com/AuthorBerylCrosherSegers
twitter.com/berylsegers @berylsegers
instagram.com/berylcroshersegers @berylcroshersegers

www.ingramcontent.com/pod-product-compliance
Lightning Source LLC
Chambersburg PA
CBHW032151080426
42735CB00008B/670